SUZANNE EVANS

THE HELL YEAH DIARIES

Uncensored Outbursts on the Path to 7-Figures

Hell Yeah Publishing

Murrells Inlet, South Carolina

DEDICATIONS

To Mom, for always telling me to get my ass in the game.

To Dad, for teaching me how to grow things.

To Amanda, for keeping it all in perspective.

To Melonie, for being the Hell No to all my Hell Yeahs.
(A girl needs that.)

CONTENTS

ACKNOWLEDGEMENTS

I acknowledge everything because it got me here and it helped to get this book in your hands.

(Sorry, if you were expecting me to do a traditional acknowledgement you obviously don't know me very well. I don't play by the rules).

INTRODUCTION TO INTRODUCTIONS

This is where I tell you a bit about myself, my philosophy, and set the stage for some of the bigger themes you'll want to pay attention to.

It's also where I warn you that if you are offended by expletive language you should probably return this book now and get your money back (Unless of course you purchased an autographed copy in which case you're shit out of luck).

1

INTRODUCTIONS

The original manuscript for this book is taken from a collection of blog and newsletter posts for my original business, Help More People, and my current business, Suzanne Evans Coaching. Some of the content has been reworked, updated, and rethought to make it more relevant for the business community at large.

The book is designed so that you can either read straight through from introduction to the final chapter, or, if you're inclined to just say, "Fuck it*" and read as you want, you can pick and choose the essays that speak to you the most (I've never played by the rules so I say do what works for you).

This book is the culmination of over 4 years of insights, a-has, breakthroughs, breakdowns, and a whole host of educational learnings taken while building a multiple 7-figure business from scratch. If you want to know my complete story of how I went from secretary to 7-figure business owner, feel free to skip over to the chapter titled, "Here's why I went into business."

I'll be honest: This book feels in many ways like a cathartic cleansing—my clearing the path of all the thoughts, random ideas, half-baked notions and other insights into building a business that both helps other and makes a shit load of money. Some think you can't have both, that somehow you need to intrinsically sacrifice your core being in order to make a profit. Not only do I think that's nonsense, but I also know that the more money you make, the more you can help people.

You can't change the world from a trailer park. But you can change the world from a rented deluxe mobile home if you choose.

It's my intention to share with you how you can make your dreams come true.

Enjoy some ranticles.

—Suzanne Evans
February 17, 2012

*My partner Melonie asked me if I was going to be able to make it through the introduction of this book without dropping the f-bomb. Sorry babe.

LET'S STOP THIS RUMOR

There is a nasty rumor in the business world.

The rumor is that coaches, healers, helpers, and anyone who wants to make money while making a difference aren't serious about business. I hear it all the time and there are some facts to back it up.

Typically, helping professions earn less, focus less on numbers, and carry more debt.

According to Forbes.com, the salary of a life-coach is six figures for only 10 to 20 percent of coaches. Since the median salary for life coaches in the United States is only $30,000 to $40,000 per year, it means that there are a lot of coaches who are making much less than $30,000.

I want to be the rumor crusher. I'm going to be the one who tells you that if you want to buck the trends mentioned above, you're going to have to get real. You're going to have to be willing to watch numbers, You're going to have to be a serious business owner and not a hobbyist.

Here are my "GET REAL, No Bullshit Rules of Business." Follow these and you will make a fortune and make a difference!

There are no refunds for being lazy.

Just because I am a coach doesn't mean I am responsible for you to show up, work hard, or succeed. We actually have people ask us to refund them for a program if they did not use it. This is not Wal-Mart. I want every one of you to have a refund policy and stick by it and stick to it. All businesses have policies, and because we "help" people does not mean it is our responsibility to have someone show up for a call or open a notebook. I did my part. I created the product and delivered the program clients have to do theirs. There are no refunds for being lazy.

If you have to say you are conscious, you may not be.

There is a lot of conscious entrepreneur talk going around. It's never a good idea to fly your "conscious" flag. How about you stop worrying about the labels, work hard, make lots, give back, and let others call you "conscious"? Focus on the goal: to have a profitable business. Conscious is a title you get, not one you give yourself. If you use your money to make a difference in your life and others, you will be more than conscious.

Know the definition of business.

The definition of business is an economic system in which goods and services are exchanged for one another or money, on the basis of their perceived worth. Every business requires some form of investment and a sufficient number of customers to whom its output can be sold at profit on a consistent basis.

Business is profit. Business is not to make you feel good, others feel good, build community, or otherwise. It is great when it does those things. That is a side effect and a beautiful one, but when you put those above profit you will struggle. You will make this hard and you will go broke. Profit first, then all the other missions.

You can only save so much.

You have to invest to make a business work. From Day One I spent money in and on my business. I worked two jobs to do it. You can decide where it comes from, but you better have a financial foundation for your business:

1) day job
2) loan
3) credit
4) spouse support
5) current revenue
6) savings.

Have a plan to SPEND money in your business. It takes investment.

Don't throw like a girl.

There is a lot of feminine energy talk these days. I am all for feminine energy and masculine energy and all energies, but don't let it be your primary message. People want results. They want a plan. They need to pay their bills, lose weight, get clients, or be happy. Talk results; not concepts.

Be pissed off regularly.

If you are still reading this, you may not hate me yet. But I get pissed off a lot and in a good way. I use that to teach, to share, and to stop people from making the same mistakes I did. Use your opinions, don't hide them. People need more truth in business.

Get real or go home.

This is business. This is entrepreneurship and it's not for the faint of heart. It is not for everybody, and frankly, many people I meet should not go into business. They can have a big impact on the world in multiple ways, but being a business owner is not their best path.

Be serious. Be ready. Be willing. Be committed.

Business is one of the most beautiful (and scary) journeys you will ever take. Get real or go home.

MAKE A DIFFERENCE

A series of global and economic changes puts us in a new age of entrepreneurship - thank goodness. New ways of doing business are emerging and some sales/ business has dried up and some has truly flourished. There is a difference. I want you to know what is working and how you can build, and build while others are scrambling to figure out what went wrong.

There are three very key ways to make a difference and make money right now. Do all three and you WILL make millions while making a difference.

1) Listen.

Many business owners keep selling (or pushing) their products/services and they are not awakened to the fact that people have changed—especially in the last few years—and want different things. There is a different need and desire to make lasting change, And if you just sell and do not listen, you are not aiming to make a difference. Ask your clients what they want most and pay close attention to what is not said. You cannot make money selling what you think people need. Listen to what they want and be ready to change, adapt, or grow.

2) Get Live.

The technology gauntlet has swung. There are so many x-boxes, iPads, tweets, and texts that people are starving for human contact. How can you connect with people one-on-one? There is no better way to make that deep connection and find out how you can help people. Plan a time to take people to lunch, host drinks at an event you are attending, do a one day event, find a local expo—and networking, networking, networking always works when you work it.

Live and in person IS the new social networking trend.

3) Pick up the phone.

The best (please hear me out on this one—no pun intended) BEST way to close sales and get clients right now is picking up the phone and speaking to people. You must make a connection and ASK for the sale. Take 100% responsibility for your offerings and for helping people. If you are looking to fill a program or get clients on a kitchen timer for 15 minutes, brainstorm a list of 25 people, then pick up the phone, show them how you can help, and ASK for the sale. Don't hide behind your computer. Connect and ask!

To truly make a difference and make millions, use the NEW way to love clients up and be of service: Go back to basics. People want YOU. So get off your ass and connect now.

DO YOU KNOW WHY?

There is a movement inside you. It might be sleeping, but it is present. We are each born with a movement to make a difference and have an impact, and the way we share that becomes our medium. Some will teach, others coach, some support, or volunteer. I think the greatest tragedy in life is not sharing your movement or your unique ability with others and the world.

From that movement is your deep seated WHY, or what I call your "so that."

Do you want to make a million dollars? Why? It's just a number. Why do you want 20 clients? It's just a number. But when you understand your WHY, your "so that," your legacy no longer becomes a number. It becomes a mission. And when you are on a mission, money is easy. I know that might tick some of you off, but it is. It flows. It shows up. Opportunities expand and grow without your hard work.

So, you must get clear.

☞ **WHY are you in business?**

☞ **WHAT do you want to change?**

☞ **WHAT legacy will your business leave behind? and...**

☞ **FOR WHOM?**

In the words of P Diddy, "Don't chase the paper. Chase the dream."

I have a dream for women and men to have no shame about money. They are empowered by making money because they know they are the global thought leaders in the world that will use that money to create change and positive growth. I want the right people making millions because I know they will make a difference. I know my legacy is to give people the hope of being financially free through their business and the specific formula to get there. I know my legacy is to help make millionaires that have legacies that will share that wealth to live their own abundant lives and share that with others.

When you know your WHY, you can ask anyone to work with you. No fear.

When you understand your legacy—you are driven to make money. No fear.

When you are clear about what you want to change none of this feels like work.

No fear.

If you have been struggling with your business or making money (even a little) knowing and owning your legacy will set you free.

WHAT IF WE STOPPED MARKETING?

I am trying to be as real with you as I can. (Honesty is my strong suit.) A lot of marketers and coaches have been lying to you. Now, I do believe that most of them have not done it intentionally. They forgot or are so focused on their position they have ignored their own facts.

So, I ask the question, what if we stopped marketing?

If we stopped marketing we might all be surprised. All the hype about passive income, sitting on the beach while you get rich, "do less to make more," or "this is the ONE system that solves everything" is just hype—it truly is. There is only one thing that will grow, propel, and sustain a 6-, 7-, or 20-figure business: a movement! So, all the drama of marketing is just that—drama.

To make a difference and make money, stop marketing and start a movement.

OK, now let's cover some basic questions:

Stop marketing?

Well, of course marketing serves a role in your business, and you need to market on some level. But marketing alone and first is not going to solve your problems. It is just a spoke in the wheel. Creating a movement is the lynchpin; it is where you start.

What is a movement?

\ím¸v-ment\ An ongoing, informal group action that is inspired by a passionately shared idea and directed toward positive change

Friends, it is not what is in your emails, auto-responders, or strategy that attract people to you. It is your passion-ately-shared idea directed towards for positive change. Building a business is not rocket science like many would like to scare you into believing; it is heart science. But, there are a few major pitfalls to avoid:

- A confusing message/movement

- Keeping your movement a secret—not sharing your message and leaving the house to spread the idea

- Thinking you do not have to ask people to join

- Giving up

Just look around you (both in and outside your own industry) at who has become a huge success. It was all about movements—not marketing—that launched these folks:

- Ali Brown created a new wave of communication— the email newsletter—to reach more people.

- Dr. Oz transformed scary doctor talk into table talk and got a nation healthy.

- David Neagle took complicated universal laws and simplified them for inspiration and optimum wealth.

- Rosa Parks simply had enough, and in an hour, created the Civil Rights Movement.

- Lance Armstrong turned cancer into courage

Folks, marketing helped these ideas get out, but it did not form them. Your movement is the single most important element in your business. Is yours clear? Are you ready? What will you change? Stop marketing and start a movement.

IS THIS A HOBBY?

Heart-centered entrepreneurs (lovingly referred to as "Helpingpreneurs") want to help. Imagine that. You have a giving heart and a spirit of support, healing, and love. **Often times that beauty stops you from putting business first**. And business first is really important.

My colleague Gina Ratliffe has a poignant question for service professionals:

"Are you a hobbyist, or Are you wealth conscious?"

The wealth-conscious entrepreneur understands that values, standards, and efficiency not only serve your business model, but also serve your clients and customers.

Do you know the answers to these questions?

◆ Is your business running organically and a little on the fly?

◆ Do you have policies, guidelines, and procedures in place?

You cannot imagine how knowing the answers to these questions will improve your effectiveness and your clarity.

Here are five must haves to make sure you are a wealth-conscious entrepreneur and not just a hobbyist.

1. Honor your Commitments

In business your commitment is your word. Be on time, be ready, and over deliver. I have actually had a coach not show up for calls. Now, we all make a mistake, but follow through, show up, and deliver.

If you have a product going out, be certain it goes out on time. If you are delivering a service, make certain it is as promised. You may gloss these over as obvious, but stop and think: Am I honoring every commitment at the absolute highest level?

2. Set an Example

I read a great quote the other day: "Your sermon is best told by your life and not your lips." Make certain you are modeling the positive image for your business and services. Your appearance, presence, energy, and language all represent YOU. It is easy to get busy in the day to day and forget what we are sharing. Sometimes it can be the smallest thing that someone picks up on and that is the image they carry forever. Preach through your actions and your words.

3. Run it Like a Business

When you are in the service industry, the same best-practices apply. You do not avoid policies, efficiencies, and procedures because your business is helping and supporting others. To truly help and support, you run your business clean and clear. Have policies, have your team and your clients understand them, and have them in writing. Keep all conversations and communication on a business level and remind yourself why you are running this business. If you are here to serve, then make sure your business is serving everyone's highest interest by being clear and well informed.

4. Have a Mentor

When you have a seasoned person to ask for guidance and support, everything is easier. One of my mentors always says, "Business is messy" and it can be, so to have someone to use as a sounding board, to ask, and to advise is leveraging your best interests in business growth. I am telling you, MENTORS. I don't leave home without them.

5. Be Uncomfortable (repeat as needed)

Change is good, not always easy. And it is not always comfortable, but it means something is shifting, and we are moving. Being uncomfortable in your business and stretching yourself beyond the comfort zone means you are NOT in hobby mode. **Begin to worry if everything is perfect, and you are care free!** It is in the discomfort that we risk, journey, and leap!

Your gifts are unique and only you can share the blessing of you. Make sure you are in wealth conscious business mode. It will serve you, your clients, your success, and your income growth.

START A MOVEMENT

Pardon me as I shift into "Preacher Mode."

(This is where I imagine myself standing before you almost as part of my congregation.).

Feel free to shout out "Hell Yeah" as needed.

It's stirring inside of me right now to the point that I cannot stop writing, thinking, talking, and sharing about it. I think we all got fooled, lost track, or lost faith. Something went wrong in the marketing madness and the frenzy of buys, sales, promotions, and launches.

Now, I do not want anyone getting me wrong.

The only way to make business and money is to sell your services. The way to spread your message is to market. They work and they are necessary, but they are tools, not strategy. They are tools, not the gift to share.

In all of the marketing hype and sales solutions, we have lost sight of our most singular purpose and the skills that allow us to help more people: The movement inside of us to be the change, to shape the world, and to help more people.

Do you know your message?

Do you understand the purpose you are to live and share with others?

I have been asking people, and they are getting a bit stuck. I see they put all their focus on the ezines, the sales copy, blogging, and social media. They focused on learning skills and left behind the calling to serve. Again, don't get me wrong. I am not shutting down my Twitter account; what better way to get my message out! But, I have to put the message before the marketing. I have to launch the movement above the business model.

Stop marketing... just for a moment. Can you hear what you are here to change? Pause. Clarify. Identify why.

Stop Marketing. Start a Movement.

HERE'S WHY I WENT INTO BUSINESS

It was 2007. I was working a day job on Broadway. One night I was looking over my credit card statements and decided to fill out a budget sheet to see how long it would take to pay off my debts. I almost cried when I saw it would take 21 years.

Right there I had to make a choice: I could "live smaller" and be afraid of money and wealth, or I could find a way to double my income. I knew my day job (which, quite frankly, after ten years had left me unsatisfied) would never give me the lifestyle I needed to become the person I always knew I could be. I wanted to make a mark. I wanted to leave a legacy, and though I didn't know what to do, what I did know was that I had to do something, and quick.

Necessity sprung me to action.

Before we move forward there are some things you should know about me:

- I failed math. **Twice.** F+

- I had no formal business training.

- I launched my business from my 350-square-foot apartment. I♡NYC

How did I do it? I started by looking at my gifts, my talents, and what I like to call "my mess." Later, I would start to recognize it as part of my "movement."

I knew that I was always great at helping people. So, I decided to become a life coach. I went to school and got trained, all while working a 60-hour-a-week day job.

Armed with my certification, I gleefully opened my doors for business, only to find no one waiting to come in.

What happened next was probably the most humbling yet beautiful gift that I have ever received since becoming an entrepreneur.

I decided to hold a speaking gig. four people showed up.

I remember crying in the bathroom, ready to give up. I remember telling myself this was "too hard." I remember pulling into my driveway, and as I was drying my eyes, I looked up and asked myself if I was taking myself too damn seriously.

In that moment I DECIDED to get over myself and start focusing on who I wanted to help. And in that moment it became clear that TENACITY is the most important trait you can have in business.

Next step was Whole Foods (and not just for lunch). I knew that if I was going to succeed I'd have to do things differently. While stopping at Whole Foods I looked around at all the little "tasting booths" and thought, "Why not have a booth for life coaching?" I asked the manager if he'd let me sell to his customers. With his blessing, the next thing I knew I was sitting in the produce section between the bananas and tomatoes offering advice. **The best part? I got clients from it.**

From there it became incredibly clear that for me to succeed, I'd have to master marketing and sales. I also realized that I needed to find a way to turn my own "mess" into a serious business to help other people.

Turning my "mess into my message" helped me quickly build a multi-six-figure business. Then something funny happened: Other entrepreneurs wanted to know how I did it. And they wanted to pay me to have me teach them. It's why in 2008 I started Help More People, a company designed to help people make millions while making a difference.

The goal was simple: to help women entrepreneurs get rid of their shame around money, marketing, and sales, so that they can build businesses that leave a legacy while making a fortune.

Business was good. I launched four businesses in four months making hundreds of thousands of dollars. Refusing to shy away from confrontation or "play by the rules" I quickly earned a reputation for being a bit "in your face" while many of the other coaches out there took a softer approach.

Nice girls don't talk that way!

I took to the stage, breaking the industry tradition of waiting years before speaking in public. It became very clear that my message of making a difference while making money resonated with many women (and even a few men) entrepreneurs. Rather than try to be something I thought people might want, I was committed to being myself: funny, sarcastic, with a dash of tough love.

On my first sold-out national tour I taught hundreds of entrepreneurs the secrets to stop marketing and start a movement.

Over the next 12 months, business grew by over 110%, sending us past seven figures and helping Suzanne Evans Coaching to become one of the fastest growing companies in America.

In 2010, I launched my first annual Be the Change seminar, a one-of-a-kind experience where hundreds of women entrepreneurs combine marketing, wealth building, and philanthropy to create a life of money and meaning.

I now offer a multitude of programs and private coaching packages all designed to help entrepreneurs create the life they want. I pride myself on my deep compassion mixed with no-nonsense advice (despite the occasional request for me to stop cursing).

Beyond making money for both myself and my clients, my next big goal is help give back those in need.

2
FACING THE FACTS

The is where I (not so) politely ask you to drop the bullshit and get clear on what's holding you back from living the life and building the business you want.

DOES YOUR BUSINESS HAVE VALUES?

I first realized the importance of a value-based company when I visited Zappos and was inspired by a business that operates daily off of a specific set of values to serve the company and the customers. It really got me thinking about my own values for Suzanne Evans Coaching and how living those values daily serves my clients, my subscribers, and my life.

We often get so busy marketing, strategizing, and serving that we don't take the time to identify our core values for the business. I think this is one of the most important visions I have created for myself lately and when you can stay on track with your business values, you naturally help more people and make more money.

It is really key to have them in writing so that you can be reminded of your purpose. We all get busy, overwhelmed, and frustrated. When your mission gets marginalized by life, you can revisit these and get back on track.

Here are the values of Suzanne Evans Coaching. I am proud to say that I strive to work and live by these daily, as does my support team.

1. Always more. Provide all that we can to change people's lives and businesses: More support, more help, more love, more gratitude, and more accountability. Keep providing MORE.

2. Gratitude. Take time to be thankful in every transaction and with every client..

3. Equality. Treat every client, customer, and subscriber with the same high level of support, service, and love no matter which package or program they participate in.

4. Own it. We are 100% responsible for all that happens at Suzanne Evans Coaching. The good, the bad, wins, losses, mistakes, and opportunities. Own all of it.

5. Model. Be a model for those we serve by never giving up, always learning, and supporting people unconditionally.

6. Think Big. Playing small does not serve anyone. We can only help more people if we are raising our standards, our vision, and our own bar for success.

7. Play. What's the point of anything if not fully, deeply, and richly enjoyed? Play more!

8. Be fearless. Even in the face of uncertainty and possible failure, we do it anyway. Embracing fear is the key success component.

9. Ask. Always ask what our clients and customers want. Be on a continual quest to over serve.

19. Honesty. Tell the truth even when it loses us money, time, or resources. Be an open company that values integrity.

A defined and specific set of values can be one of the best ways you serve your clients, market your services, and change the world!

ARE YOU TELLING THE TRUTH?

Many of you are lying to yourself. You have been for a while.

Don't get huffy. You know it's true and it isn't intentional, but it is happening. I see it day, after day, after day. Usually it shows up in the form of …

Unfulfilled promises

Commitments not kept

The use of "Things Change" to disguise deals broken

Quitting.

I know, this isn't the most uplifting concept ever shared, but if you will take it to heart, it might be just the one to change your life and your business. I have spent a lot of time studying two things:

Great speakers

The truth.

Both interest me greatly and are the next steps for where I am about to go in my business path. I have found that most people are unhappy, and most businesses unsuccessful for the exact same reason: People are not being truthful.

So, here are down-and-dirty steps to getting real, getting honest, and getting ahead fast. Use these rules in business and in life. They are interchangeable.

1. Do what you say you are going to do whatever you have committed to honor it at all costs … whether that commitment was made to yourself, or to someone else. Lie enough to yourself and others, and nothing you say will hold weight. Do what you say you will do.

2. Do it when you say you will do it. Don't be late (literally and figuratively) and if you are, don't make excuses. Do it when you say you will. No one wants to work with someone unpredictable. Period.

3. Do it how you said you would do it & don't half-ass anything. The way you show up and deliver is the exact way you will increase your revenue and your lifestyle.

4). Don't be cheap and tell yourself you are frugal. Stay in a nice place, tip well, fly first class, give to others, and invest deeply in yourself.

5. A deal is a deal. One of my favorite motivators/ coaches right now says people that "break deals" are liars (his words not mine, but I do agree) If you over committed—oops! If you overextended—ick! If you took on too much—whoops. It doesn't matter. A deal is a deal. You honor all deals, verbal, written, and promised.

6. Make a decision. Indecision is a form of self-abuse. There are only about 2% of things in life we actually ever need to "think" over. We know what we need to do. We are just too chicken to do it, so we wait. Make a decision and move on.

7. Balance does not equal procrastination. All the time I hear, "I will not work that hard, I will not go that far or that long because I want to maintain balance." Don't fool yourself into thinking that doing less is "balance." The most balanced people I know are really hard workers. They do what they love, many for 10-12 hours a day. They have great support, they delegate the things they hate, and they play harder than they work. Balance is joy. Balance is not how hard you do or do not work.

I could go on and on, and I may. But the bottom line is that the truth will set you free. Know that building a business and life of your dreams takes effort, commitment, and energy. The more real you get, the more success you can attain.

WHERE YOU ARE RIGHT NOW IS WHERE YOU HAVE CHOSEN TO BE

Take a moment to think about that. Depending on where you are, this may feel amazing, but it might not feel so great.

Your mindset is an incredibly important part of the business-building game. Moreover, it is directly related to the impact that you're going to have in this world.

There are five basic questions you must ask yourself when building a business or looking to take an existing business to the next level. These are all related to mindset.

1. Are you afraid of messing up?

In other words, are you waiting to take action because you don't want to fail?

2. Is building your business really overwhelming?

Do you find yourself not knowing where to start sometimes or maybe even a lot of the time?

3. Do you compare yourself to others?

This one's really important. Do you find yourself comparing yourself to what's coming into your inbox? Are you looking at what other people have in their e-zines or what they have accomplished and basing your self-worth off of that?

4. Do you believe (without hesitation) that you have the ability to make multiple 6-figures and beyond?

5. Are you so certain in your sales conversion calls that you close at over 90%?

If you answered yes to #1, #2, or #3, or no to #4 or #5 (essentially negative responses implying a lack of confidence in your business), it is time to take a hard look at your belief system in regards to building your business, because today you decide where you will be in the very near future. It is up to you.

First, it is important to know that there is no competition. People often come up to me and say that they really want to do something, but there are so many other people already doing it, that they aren't sure if it's what they should do.

What people quite frequently forget is that there can only be one YOU! Do you know how many marketing and mindset coaches there are out there? There are hundreds, if not thousands, if not tens of thousands of them out there, but there is no one doing it like me. There is no one else doing it Suzanne-Evans style (and God bless them if they try). Likewise, no one can do what you do like you can.

Let go of the idea of competition. There is no competition. The only competition you will find is a manufactured competition that you have created.

Another issue people have related to mindset is that they wait for everything to be "just right" to launch a product or to even start their business at all. This kind of perfectionism holds people back from helping people, making money, and really making a difference in the world.

There's a great Marianne Williamson quote that says, "Your playing small doesn't serve the world. It also doesn't serve your family, your spouse, or your church, or your community, or your friends."

I often hear people saying, "I would do this, but I have to take care of my 95-year-old mother," or "I would do this, but I have three toddlers at home," or many other excuses beginning with "I would do this, but..."

By playing small, not being in the right mindset, not asking for clients, not marketing yourself, or putting all the pieces together, you are being a terrible example for your children, community, family, friends, etc. When you are a leader and you step up and build a business that makes a difference in this world, you change everyone's mindset, and indeed you change the world.

So many people want to change the world but fail to realize that the only person they can directly change is themselves. You must start with your own mindset. Your sales conversions, your ability to make money, whether or not you are comparing yourself to others or not, and any uncertainty that you're experiencing are all reflections of your belief in what is possible for you.

A quick commentary on the word "mindset." Please note I use two words when describing this because "mindset" because is really about getting your mind "set" in the right way. Treat your belief in yourself like a thermostat and not a thermometer. You set it where you want it to be.

When I realized and began implementing this, clients literally started finding me. My belief in myself was firm. People want to be around that. No one wants to surround themselves with uncertainty and insecurity.

Continually ask yourself, "How am I showing up?" People are attracted to authority, and authority inspires!

IS YOUR BUSINESS PORTFOLIO BROKE?

I am no expert in the stock market and I certainly do not claim to be, but this I know: To make OR lose money in the market, you have to invest in the market. It goes back to the saying, "You got to be in it to win it." So take a moment and think about this. Seriously—grab pen and paper.

How much do you spend on your car every year? (payment, insurance, tune-ups, gas, etc.)

Okay, got that number?

Take a long look at it. If you are spending a similar amount or LESS on your business, take a pause. How do we expect to have thriving businesses and help more people if we spend more on our cars than on our passions? It's scary! I remember the first time I did this, and it was a real eye opener. I quickly realized that if I do not treat my business coaching, programs, workshops, and seminars as investments in me, my future, and those I want to serve, then my business would never grow. The first year I took this idea and applied it, making investments in myself via coaching, programs, and building a team, my income doubled. Here's the best part—the number of people I was serving more than quadrupled. When we invest in ourselves, we build a portfolio for success.

Many people ask me (actually, a client just asked me this morning) about how to determine the BEST investment for business. It is not a cut-and-dried formula since there are so many variables in business, but there are some integral components that you should include:

◆ An authentic marketing program where you get one-on-one attention.

◆ Opportunities where you will be with other business owners that you can partner with.

◆ Programs or coaching that PULL you. In other words, programs or coaching in which you can just feel the possibility.

◆ Programs where you are mentored by people who are where you want to be.

◆ Workshops/Events that just raise your JOY level and are fun.

◆ Programs that provide a full and fair guarantee.

What and how you invest will be different for each person, but investing is the key. A car cannot run without gas, a stock cannot rise without being purchased and a business cannot run without investment fuel. You must be ready and willing, financially, to invest money in and on your business.

Sometimes this means being certain you have a cash flow from other means until your business is soaring. You may want to build WHILE in a job (this is what I did) or have a part-time job, creating a savings to use for up to a year, or any other plan. But, have a financial plan to invest in your business portfolio.

With our economy and stock market all over the place these days, the only SURE investment is the one you make in YOU. You always know what your return will be. You can always go back to what you learned or the experiences. It will grow immediately. Investing in yourself is a certain way of growing financially and personally.

Over the past three and a half years I've invested over $500,000 in my business. Let me be clear. I don't mean business expenses. I mean investments: coaching, events, programs, education and resources. That investment has come back tenfold. Your key to success is believing that you are worth it and investing in your greatest asset: YOU and YOUR BUSINESS.

YOU CAN'T BE BOTH!

I had a need to be right for a long time—maybe about 30 years. Want to know what it did for me? It kept me in a job I hated, where my max earning was about $50k, I had no free time, and had created a situation where I could hardly make any of my own decisions. It became clear to me that being right no longer served me. I went as far as to have the belief that I wasn't really interested in seeking therapy or coaching. Period. I realize I was deeply afraid they might make me "wrong."

Some people will get tired of it. They will see that holding on to assumptions, ideas, and the need to be right will not get them to their desired life. Thank God I got sick and tired and was willing to let go. Honestly, the #1 reason I see entrepreneurs struggle, suffer, and often quit is because they hold onto the need to be right.

You cannot have a new life, more business, or growth without being willing to stretch and be called out on the BS. I have heard many mentors say it to me over the last four years, but I think it was Ali Brown that I first heard say, "Do you want to be right, or do you want to be rich?" You can't hold onto both desires.

Growing a business, changing your life, getting clients, and making money all take sacrifice. Sacrifice is doing something you have never done to get something you have never had.

You can't sacrifice AND need to hold onto to being right. That's why I'm going to share with you my list of Suzanne Evans patented "most frequently-done things to sabotage your success and not make more money, help more people, and have an impact because you need to be right" expressions!

Make sure you clean this list up and move into openness, willingness, and readiness to CHANGE!

1. "YES, BUT." Just remove it from your vocabulary. I have my private clients take improv class, because the #1 rule of improv is "YES!" Start changing your "Yes, but" to "YES, YES!" "Yes, but" will keep you stuck in your excuses around time, money, and knowledge.

REFRAME: "YES! YES! Anything worth doing is worth doing poorly to start with!"

2. "I QUIT." This is always the easiest answer. It can be quick and it gets you out of pain ... fast! But, guess what? Nothing changes.

REFRAME: "I get exactly what I need when I need it. Is quitting going to move me closer to my dreams?"

3. "I DIDN'T GET WHAT I NEEDED." Blame is evil. I know, because I did it. It makes us feel better when it isn't out fault. But again, it doesn't move us forward or change our outcomes.

REFRAME: "I am 100% responsible for everything that happens, good, bad, or in between."

4. "THERE ISN'T ENOUGH (Time, Money, Resources, Help)." When we are working from lack, we get lack.

REFRAME: "Everything I need is already present. And there is more than enough."

5. "THAT HURT MY FEELINGS" or **"I DON'T LIKE HOW THAT MADE ME FEEL."** Feelings are choices, so when we choose hurt or negativity, we send that energy out into the world and cause a ripple effect.

REFRAME: "I choose how I feel about everything. No one can make me feel anything. That is my choice. So, if I am offended the offense is within me."

6. "I'M NOT LISTENING." Many of you are working with coaches or in programs, but not willing to really do what is required of you or fully listen to their guidance.

REFRAME: "I have chosen this person or this path for a reason and I am willing to do what is required, even if I don't understand how or it might make me wrong." When we step up to self-responsibility in all we do, we eliminate the need to be right. We eliminate the fear of sacrifice. To truly help more people, you have to be willing to help yourself. To be the change in the world, you have to change. And it starts with being okay with letting go. If we can let go of being right and not care who gets the credit, then we can change the world over, and over, and over again.

MAKE A QUANTUM LEAP IN YOUR BUSINESS

To quantum leap in business, YOU must take 100% responsibility for everything. Did I mention everything? E_V_E_R_Y_T_H_I_N_G!

The Universal Laws prove that the world is not happening to us; we create our world. And from that creation we design, live, and choose how we operate in business. For a while I was a business owner that did fine. I understood marketing, I took action, and I made 50-60K in my business. I was unconsciously making some good decisions, but most of the decisions I was making for life and business were based in "do I have enough money to cover that?" It seemed very sensible, and on some level I was aware that it was slow going... because I was living in lack.

How can you quantum leap if every decision is based in what you DO NOT have?

My mentor said something that changed my life and if you will embrace and live it. It will change yours, too:

"You don't need the money until you make the DECI-SION to do it or have it,"

So, the conversation goes...

- I would love that house, but I can't afford it.

- I would love to go there, but I don't have the money.

- I need a coach or program, but I need to make money first.

The problem is, that's not how universal law works. The money doesn't show up until you DECIDE 100% that you are buying the house, going on the vacation, or joining the program. And some of you reading this are going, "Yes, right... nice philosophy."

Here's the deal: It works and has in my life over and over again. And when the money has not shown up (which has been rare), guess what? It was really clear I had not made the decision. Nope—had not. I was hoping the money would show up, or testing that the money would show up. When I decide and then commit fully to my energy and efforts making this happen, it works every single time. The Universe doesn't lie and it provides, but it doesn't know which support to bring until you decide.

Which decisions have you not made?

What do you REALLY want, but are waiting for the money to show up to get or have?

When I began truly embracing and understanding that I didn't need the money until I made the decision the order of my life went "house, quitting my job, freedom, my dream boat, living in three places a year, serving thousands to have the same freedom, a team of support." And you can bet I am making new decisions every day based NOT on what I have in the bank, or even what I am projecting to have in the bank, but on what I want.

Place your order. The Universe is waiting.

Then DECIDE.

Then ACT.

3

WHAT DO YOU BELIEVE?

This is where I ask you to get clear on what you really believe is possible for your business and even get a little vulnerable on you.

DO YOU BELIEVE ENOUGH TO GET NEW CLIENTS?

You have to believe in what you offer to sell what you offer.

It is the self doubt and shyness about sharing our gifts that most often keeps our rates low and new clients at bay. Every marketing tool in the world is useless without a deep knowledge and understanding that you can make a difference, what you do is needed and the gifts you have MUST be shared.

Just recently (at the time of this printing), I had a client just raise her rates significantly. She was scared, a little insecure, but she knew and I knew that her value was not aligned with the lower rates, and that her gifts are extraordinary. She just booked a new client at her new rate for a three-month contract. How? Why? It was about two things: belief and knowing.

Belief. Belief is when you must share what you do. You wake up in the morning and are compelled to market because your message is that important. Your ability to change outcomes is that powerful. You must embrace the knowing that people need you, they are waiting, and this is your time. When you believe, your clients believe. When you believe, new clients see that and want more. When you believe, people are attracted to you, and good comes through you. When you believe, marketing becomes natural and just flows.

Knowing. Knowing that it takes clearing the cobwebs and doubt in your own mind to move other people forward. Are you knowing in your services? Are you knowing that to be a leader, you must be a model? How can we truly launch others into success, healing, or movement if we are standing still? What is keeping you back from knowing that your gifts are valuable? And please hear me loud and clear: If you are feeling this way, you do not need more training or education. You need a rebirth of the empowerment of just how special, unique, and transformative you are. You need a new certification, a certification of certainty that you know enough and you are enough. Now go, do good work.

Please don't wait to share your gifts and help more people. We all need you.

CLARITY IS THE SECRET TO SUCCESS

What are you asking for? When you go to a drive-thru (for me, it's Starbucks, thank you!) do you say, "Give me what you want me to have," or "I'll take maybe a this or maybe a that?" Nope! And if you did, who the heck knows what you would get later? You think it through, decide, ask, and it is given.

It's the same with your business and success!

This week I had a client that was frustrated. She is such a lovely human being. You meet her, you melt, and you want more. I could feel she was distant and—long story short—as we spoke, and as her concerns were voiced, magic happened.

She needed more foundations, wanted some opportunities, and had some specific concerns. Once she was clear and asked for those things—BOOM! I began to rattle off everything we were going to give her, programs I was going to send her, and some specific paths to exposure.

I have to admit, I could tell she was a little surprised and then actually delighted! Ask, and it is given! Every time.

But that giving has to start first from clarity. She had to know she needed more, she had to step up and ask, and here is the best part: YOU DON'T HAVE TO HAVE THE ANSWER! You just need to be clear about asking.

She had no idea about the outcome; frankly, I think she may not have known there could be one of high value, BUT she asked. Also, she took me up on all of it. See, many of you ask, then it is given, and you say, "Oh, no, that's not it. I want something else," or "This must not be the answer." When you ask, and opportunity appears, you must grab it! You must take that opportunity and go! Be open.

- Are you asking the Universe for help, support, and signs?

- Are you asking your coach for what you need?

- Are you asking your spouse for support?

- Are you asking your clients to live up to their potential?

What are you not asking for? Ask, and it is given.

I AM SCARED

I am scared. Yep—scared.

I know you are too. Everybody is.

I also know that many of you want to be fearless. You want to share your story, build your business leave your spouse, buy the house, leave the job.

I also know you see all those emails flooding your inbox from all the people making all those whatever figures a year—the ones flying fancy planes and sipping champagne? They are scared, too. Some of them are exaggerating their stories for you because they are frightened that if you saw who they really are—imperfect, taking out the trash, walking the dog—you might not love them anymore.

And some aren't exaggerating their stories. They just live a lot like you and me—working hard, loving our work, playing, having fun, and wanting to make a difference in the world. **But we all have one thing in common: fear.**

I remember as a child watching Jesse Jackson give a political speech where he said, "Some of your folks came over on the Mayflower; mine came over on slave ships. But we are all in the same boat now."

And we are all in the same boat now, no matter where we came from or where we are. We are all looking to make more money, make an impact, serve, and live an extraordinary life. So, I want to ask you to do something with me today: I want you to understand and recognize that you aren't that far away from where I am. You aren't any different from the people writing those emails coming into your inbox. You can live any life you want, and it's ok to be scared.

I am.

The key is: You do it afraid.

The truth is: If you are afraid you have company.

The prescription is: Do it anyway.

Any next big step is scary. Believe me, I feel like I have been on a 4-year stair climber. As my mentor says, "You change, adapt, grow!" And when you do, you see results.

Now, here is what doesn't work: You are scared and you do nothing … OR you are afraid and avoid making a decision.

Success takes action even when you are afraid. Success means being nervous and investing in yourself—being afraid and starting anyway, being scared and taking risks.

Success is in doing it afraid.

"What we fear comes to pass more speedily than what we hope." —Publilius Syrus—Moral Sayings (1st C B.C.)

4
HOW TO BE UNIQUE & STAND OUT

OK, it's game time. Here's where we stop philoso-
phizing, roll up our sleeves and work up a sweat
as I show you how to grow your business without
compromising who you are.

I'VE NEVER FIT IN

And I refuse to try.

The first 30 years of my life, I did try. I didn't really know any different.

I skipped slumber parties at seven if it was the same night as 60 Minutes. And at six, I gave a political speech for Geraldine Ferraro. None of my friends knew who she was. As I grew older I couldn't have cared less about high school drama and instead spent the summers training as a professional water skier. And I had started a professional acting career when I was four.

Don't get me wrong. I wanted to hang with the cool kids and I did; I could hang out with anybody. I like people, so I got along with the nerds, hung out with the preps, and week-ended with the dreadlocked hippy group at school.

But I never really fit anywhere.

I would try. I was extremely malleable, so I would shift and change and try to be whoever I needed to in that moment. It never really worked.

I have been overweight since I was five. I have been bossy since 3. I have been the girl who does a little of everything forever. I wasn't fitting in. And I floundered between it bothering me deeply and total apathy ...

Until I turned 32. I noticed I was a pretty good marketer. I saw ideas that some people didn't. I had the primal urge to rage against what everybody else was saying/ writing/selling and do it a little different. I like a good challenge. I like to poke people.

And it hit me: My marketing works because I don't fit in. And now that I am clear, I won't even try to change (not a little):

◆ I will not stop cursing.

◆ I will not behave the way you think a coach, a marketer, or a conscious entrepreneur should.

◆ I will not make you feel good by telling you BS.

◆ I will not run my business using emotional business management (because women have for years).

◆ I will not sell the way everyone else does.

◆ I will not choose to be either "feminine or masculine"

◆ I willl not choose between being heart centered or using hardcore marketing.

- ◆ I will not do what my industry does because it looks good or is polite.

But I will be me. And I don't fit in. And it works.
And I invite you to join me. I don't want you to fit in either. There is only so much room for people to fit in, and that room gets too full; all the oxygen gets drained.

So, I'll meet you in the hallway. I am easy to find—I'll be the one dropping the F-bomb.

WHY NICHING DOESN'T WORK

You typically hear in many marketing circles that the first thing you need to do is identify your niche.

This terminology of a "niche" doesn't work for me because it feels very much like, "Find a group of random people to sell to them." I've found that a better way to identify these people is to ask, "Who needs me most?" We all have a gift to share, so ask yourself, "Who needs me and my gift the most?"

This concept is part of what I call "authentic marketing" because it's got to come from your heart. It's got to be client based and heart centered for it to really work.

When you look at who needs you most and you can recognize what your ideal client is, it's also extremely important for you to be aware that you shouldn't work with everyone.

I was once at a networking group, and someone asked this gentleman, "So who's an ideal client for you?" And he answered, "Anyone breathing." That's so not the case.

If you agree with the fact that you have a unique gift, and if you try to use that gift to serve everyone, you'll quickly see that it's simply just not possible.

First of all, you can't do your job well when you try to spread yourself that thin. You just can't do everything, you can't please everybody, and you don't have the skill set and the energy to try to spread yourself that thin.

Secondly, if you really want to be powerful, find the sweet spot where you can focus on your true gift combined with delivering it to the people who need it most.

It's important to understand these prospects—these people who need you most—and develop yourself as a perceived expert. Being an expert in your field is something that you really want to work towards, not because you want to know it all, but because it is a way that you can make your clients feel comfortable and confident with you.

I have asked clients this question before: If you need brain surgery and you're given the choice of two doctors, and one doctor focuses solely on brain surgery and he's really great at it, and the other doctor does hip replacements, knee replacements, and dabbles in some brain surgery, who are you going to pick?

I hope it is obvious.

When I ask that question, it's always obvious to the person I'm asking. But we don't do that with ourselves and within our own businesses. We tend to ignore the fact that if we were looking for anything else for ourselves —from plumbers to brain surgeons to a designer—we would look for the best of the best that is specific to the area that we're working in.

We need to really relate that to ourselves, strive to be the best of the best and develop the skill sets and connections necessary to be considered an expert in our area. Then focus on the question "Who needs me most?" which will be a more useful guide in developing our businesses than stressing over finding our niche.

When you spend time delving into these areas as the apply to your business, you too will move past any fears about marketing in ways that feel uncomfortable for you and into authentic marketing that naturally attracts your ideal clients and builds your business.

STOP MARKETING AND TELL YOUR STORY

I teach my clients the power of telling their own story as they start their own businesses with this phrase: Your Truth Will Set Them Free. This is one of the biggest neon light mistakes that I see helping professionals make.

They believe that this has nothing to do with them: "I need to focus on the clients and what the clients need. I need to make sure that I'm looking at their problems and their struggles." They don't tell their stories.

There's nothing that I hate more than going to someone's website or reading their marketing materials and reading a bio. Everybody goes, "But I'm supposed to have a bio on my website. I'm supposed to have an 'About Me' on my website."

Bios are credentials and, for the most part, pretty boring. What is fascinating, what enables you to connect with someone, to really care about someone and discover empathy is when you tell your story. This is so vitally important when you are building relationships with potential clients.

Don't tell the Cinderella version; tell the ugly-step-sister, warped version. It is your mistakes that really are going to leverage your clients to their own success.

For example, I'll share that I did some things in the beginning of my business that—had I known what I know now—certainly would have done differently.

I worked way too hard in the beginning—way too hard! I put in a lot of hours that were not necessary. I will admit to that. I also took on every client that came my way. If I could nab them, I took them. That was something that didn't serve me well in the long run.

I also followed the marketing "gurus." I believed that if I just did everything exactly their way, it would work for me. The result was that I was exhausted, a little bit confused, and really frustrated. What happened was I didn't have a core message.

I thought, "I've got to have a name. It's got to be cute. It's got to appeal to people. It's got to be as big as Pepsi and Coca-Cola."

That only made me even more exhausted. It came to the point where I really stopped trying to create this business that seemed like a 24-story building in some imaginary business land. I just said, "This is who I am. The best thing that I have to offer is me."

Your truth will set them free. Your journey, your mistakes, how you overcame obstacles, and your conclusions, this is the insight your clients are looking for.

You know that your bio is about everything that you've accomplished. Maybe you have 67 credentials, and maybe you talk about where you went to school. Maybe it's talking about your kids or your family. (And those things are important as well. People like to hear about them.)

But what's most important is: Why you? What's your story? If you're going to work with parents having difficulties with their kids and you're going to be a parenting coach, what's your story in that? Why are you coming to this area? What do you have to bring to other parents?

Was it that you struggled at being a parent, really made a turn, and now you can share this experience with other people? Was it that you had an extraordinary parenting situation that maybe wasn't so pleasant but taught you a lot that you can now share with others?

If you're a health coach, what's your story around health? You wouldn't be drawn to something if you don't have a story it, a stake in it, or if something in your life didn't bring you to it.

If you answer, "Oh, I don't know what my story is," I ask you to really dig deep. It's there. It may be covered up, or it may be something that you're afraid to share, but it's definitely there. Share your story. It is what opens people up to wanting to work with you.

HOW TO SEPARATE YOURSELF FROM OTHERS

A common challenge for coaches, teachers, healers, and other helping professionals is differentiating themselves from others in their fields.

The good news is, you set yourself apart just by being born. People forget that. The nature of your unique life makes you different and unique. I call this your "intuitive intelligence."

You have not lived the same life that I have lived, and neither has anyone else. Even if we have the same training and we sat down and decided to teach the exact same model to people, it would be different because we are different people.

Hold your hand up in front of you right now. No one shares those finger prints. Your marketing style, your business style, and your message all reflect that uniqueness.

Get off of the marketing hamster wheel for a while and ask yourself the question: "Why did you get into this game to begin with?"

There is a reason that you are reading this chapter.

There is a reason that you're doing the business you're doing.

◆ Someone reading this lost a significant amount of weight.

◆ Someone reading this made it through a serious illness.

◆ Someone reading this helped a child through a diagnosis.

◆ Someone reading this got divorced and they thrived through it.

◆ Someone reading this changed their lifestyle through health and wellness.

◆ Someone reading this built a business out of nothing.

Continually telling my story has been the most powerful business-building strategy I have ever implemented, and it comes completely naturally because it's my story. Framing it in a way that underlines my movement and the changes I want to see in the world helps me attract perfect clients.

Everyone has a story and any business must have a movement and a mission driving it. Don't lose sight of the fact that it is your story that is going to heal people.

When I started my business, I finally got off my butt and decided to do something and change something. I came across coaching. I didn't have a clue how to market. It was hard and it was painful, and there were some really difficult pieces.

Through that experience I healed a lot in myself, I healed a lot in other people, and I now have this really brilliant gift. I know that my purpose on this earth is to help people heal their shame around money and use marketing and business building as the tools to do that.

Keep it simple. Go back to the reason you got into your business or the field you're in to begin with, whether you are an energy worker, a life coach, or a marketing consultant. Why did you start this to begin with? Because that's what you've lost sight of if you don't have the energy to share your movement in a way that differentiates yourself from others.

ARE YOU LOOKING LEFT & RIGHT?

I used to be a professional water skier in a former life. (Don't laugh. There are pictures!) And when skiing in a lineup, it is important to keep looking straight ahead in order to keep clean lines and not run into someone. I always struggled with this. If I am talking to you, I need to look at you. Have you ever driven with someone who turns their head to talk WHILE driving? It can be scary.

I see entrepreneurs do this in business all the time. They look left and right to see what everyone else is doing. They seek out approval behind them and catch a peek to see who is ahead so they can go into "catch up" mode. And just like driving in the car, it makes for a scary situation.

And why are we looking left and right? Competition.

"Every man in the world is better than someone else and not as good someone else." —William Saroyan

No other business can be like yours. YOU are what makes your service, product, or program uniquely yours. There is no competition. I know that is hard to remember at times, and even I have found myself rushing many times to do what someone else did. I find that when I catch myself, I realize it is my own insecurity or fear sneaking up and I let it guide me. When I listen to my intuition, I know that it is just my subconscious playing tricks on me—trying to get me to believe old stories that are not true.

When I breathe and recognize what the truth is, I know that looking to the left and right does not serve me. I can only run my best race, serve my clients, and be in joy when I look straight ahead that's my goal line. So here are a few pointers to keep you from judging and comparing yourself, so that the BEST you is always present:

1. When in doubt, hold your hand up in front of you. Look at your fingertips. No one else has those. Only you. Remember, there is no competition. There is no comparison. There is only YOU. Look straight ahead.

2. Feeling behind? Stop and take stock. Can you really be behind in business? Whose rules are you following? This is a great time to look at your goals, give your vision board a makeover, or start a treasure map. This is your business, your life, your mission. You are only behind if you are doing it someone else's way.

Look straight ahead.

3. Be grateful. You simply cannot feel competitive, angry, or envious if you are in a state of gratefulness. I just grab a sheet of paper and go set a time for 10 minutes and write gratefuls until the time is up. This process simply changes your entire perspective. Look straight ahead.

You can't help more people looking left and right. Stay on purpose, look ahead, and keep changing the world!

THERE IS NO COMPETITION

Something that many coaches, healers, and other helping professionals have a hard time wrapping their mind around is the fact that there really is no competition.

There just isn't. I don't have any and I don't think about it.

Let me explain what I mean:

I'm not a horse race person, but I've seen one or two. All the horses wear blinders. They are little flaps that go beside their eyes. They do that because the minute a horse looks at the horse beside them, it slows down.

In this same way you must run your own race in business. There are a lot of people who are overwhelmed, under-performing, under-implementing, and not doing what they need to do to grow their business because they are so engrossed in all the newsletters, e-zines, and emails that are coming through their inbox making them feel "less than" magnificent.

Stop basing your value and your success on what's coming into your inbox. Shut it down, put it in a filter, and go build your business. Go run your own race. Go tell people about your story, share your message, and share your movement.

The minute you begin to compare yourself to others, or you look to others for validation, it will slow you down and the phone will stop ringing.

People always want to know how to start with nothing and go to a booming business with multiple programs and affiliates. People want to know how to get traffic to their site and more people in the door.

The answer that no one wants to hear is that there is no magic pill! The way to build a successful, sustainable business is to start talking to one person, and then you talk to two people, and then you talk to those people about how they can talk to someone.

It's the same basic process whether your focus is online or offline. About 90% of the work I do is virtual, but when you're getting started, consider using what you have in your immediate vicinity. Look to your town or your community. Regardless of where your business is or whether it is primarily online or offline, your approach must be based around connecting with more and more people.

I had a private client who once asked, "How do you get joint ventures and affiliate partners?" I told her to do it the same way you make friends!

Approach affiliate opportunities and joint ventures the same way you live your life. Just reach out to people. When you find yourself saying, "Gosh, there's something about that person that resonates for me," connect with them. There's nothing secret about it!

So many people try to put more mystery into this than there needs to be. Although it isn't complicated, you do have to put the connection time in. Nothing gets built offline or online unless you take the time, the energy, and the commitment to make connection, after connection, after connection.

The wonderful quote, "Be more interested than interesting" is relevant to this. The worst thing in the world to do when making connections or partaking in any kind of marketing activities like social media is to say something like, "Hi, I'm Suzanne! Buy my stuff!" Nobody cares!

You must walk into a business networking, marketing, or social media situation the same way you walk into a real party: Introduce yourself, talk with people, ask people about commonalities.

Walk into every room (or virtual event, or social media site) like it's your party. What would you do if it were your party? You would thank people for coming. You would ask them how they are. You would see what you could do for them. You would be more interested than interesting.

There will always being people doing what you do, and there will always be people with more experience and less experience, but one thing is for certain: There can be only one YOU. Stop looking around you and start looking up. There is a world of people that need your help and are waiting. You can't see them if you are watching other people.

5

GETTING CLIENTS

Here's where I ask you to decide if you'd like to start making money, or just want to keep talking about how you'd like to start making money.

If you'd like to start making money, you're going to love this next section.

HOW TO LEARN TO TALK TO PROSPECTS AND GET RESULTS!

People buy solutions, not services or a process. People are running a race because they want to make it to the finish line. They do the same thing in the marketplace for coaching. People seek solutions to their problems. That's the finish line for them. They seek answers to their dilemmas. If you package and offer solutions, you can relay a message that people understand and want.

This fact that people buy solutions not services and a process also really ties into your target market. When I shifted my message to the solutions I have for people's problems, it totally shifted my business.

It's easier to attract clients, and I'll tell you this, it's a heck of a lot more fun, because instead of being caught in your own process and trying to explain what your service is and how you serve your clients, you're focused on the benefits and on the finish line. That really motivates people when you're speaking to them and it's really important.

Some people in the marketing world call it your "unique selling proposition."

You need to establish who needs you most. They're a group who …

◆ Can afford you

◆ Are accessible

◆ Are already grouping together

◆ Have a problem you're clear about

◆ Have a problem with solutions you're clear about

◆ Will be receptive to the benefits and solutions you have to offer

When I first started my business I would tell people who asked about what I did that "coaching is a process in which you ask engaging powerful questions to get somebody to come to their own answers about the problems."

People's eyes were glazing over. They were like, "What?"

I did this a couple of times and I kept thinking, "Nobody gets it. Nobody is excited. Nobody's saying, 'Tell me more. Can I have a complementary session?'" Then it just hit me that I was talking about the process, and nobody really cares about the process.

So I went back and created a stress test. I decided to ask people if they want to take a stress test to see where some of the stressors are in their life. Then I was going to focus on "the benefits of coaching" and not "what coaching is."

I had people take the test, and then they would ask, "Well, tell me what coaching is."

I would say, "Do you see where you scored low on your job and that you're not really satisfied in your job? Coaching would take you from a place of dissatisfaction in your job to finding out what your real passion is and help you get excited about going to work every day. It would be creating a strategic plan to move from where you are now—unhappy in your job—to bliss in a new career."

What do you think people did? Their faces lit up, and they wanted to know more and discover where they could find this bliss. "Where do I get this new excitement in my new job?" They were excited because I was speaking to the benefits.

When you go into a networking event, try using end result benefits in describing what you do. For instance, if you work with ADHD and families you could say something like,

"You know how there are some families who have children with ADHD, and the entire family always seems overwhelmed and stressed out? They're not able to focus and really enjoy all the things in their life because all of this is so consuming.

What I do is I step in and work with those families, and take them from chaos to calm. I show them strategies, techniques, and tips so that they can all work together through the children's and maybe their own ADHD. We systematize their entire lives and family process so they can really enjoy each other and they can all be successful."

It's all about what you can help achieve for someone in pain, and not about the process or you. Keep this in mind for much more powerful results when talking to people who need what you offer.

YOU GOTTA LEAVE THE HOUSE!

The single fastest way to get clients and grow your business is to get in front of people and get in front of them IN PERSON! There is nothing like a one-on-one connection to build the know, like, and trust factor, as well as hold someone's captive attention. I am amazed how many entrepreneurs I speak with who have been trying to build their businesses from home. I know it is part of the appeal of an online/virtual business lifestyle, but starting with in-person connections builds faster and more financially-fruitful relationships. So, here are my top tips for making more money and impact by leaving the house!

1. Make certain you spend more time in front of people than in front of your computer! (Especially in the growth stages.) Making those decisions of best color for your website or researching what other people in your field are doing all have their place, but they do not directly bring you the opportunity to start a client conversation. Use the 80/20 rule: Spend 80% of your time networking, meeting, and speaking and 20% of your time on strategy and research.

2. Don't be so picky in the beginning. I hear people say they don't like this group or they are not sure if that networking organization will do anything for them. Just GO! You have no idea who someone will know or who they might be able to introduce you to. You will soon learn which groups serve you and which groups don't. But to start, just go, meet, and share your movement.

3. Don't have a drunk cowboy message. You know those people who you ask, "What do you do?" and ten minutes later you are still trying to figure out what the heck they are talking about. Be clear and concise with a two- or three-sentence message. I call this your impact statement.

4. Act like it's your party. Walk into every room as if you own it. Walk into every room as if these wonderful people have gathered here just to meet you. Greet them, be curious, ask questions, be gracious, and be in your power. People are attracted to confidence. Authority inspires.

5. Follow up and ask. Follow up with everyone you meet within 48 hours, even if it is just a quick "nice to meet you" email. Be certain to ask how you can help them and offer them a session, a freebie, or an offer to move them closer to knowing your work.

Ask for what you want a referral, an opportunity to share how you can work with them, or an alliance/ partnership.

BONUS: Have fun! You are in a service business and one of the greatest joys of this industry is meeting people and building relationships.

SPEAK FAST TO FILL YOUR BUSINESS

There are a multitude of ways to market, but some just have higher and faster impact. The #1 question I receive is, "How do I get clients?" Here is one way to do it fast and get in front of lots of people.

SPEAK! (in person)

This is the way I built my business so quickly. I spent about 70% of my marketing time looking for speaking opportunities and organizations. There are a few important steps to getting gigs, having gigs that bring in clients, and having fun!

Here are my quick tips.

1. Put the work in. You must spend research time to find places to speak. I would often carve out 2-3 hours a day of "Google" time to research organizations, opportunities, and groups in my area to speak. Here is an example:

If you are a career coach for women and you live in Raleigh, NC you might Google the following keywords: women's organizations; career associations; churches; social clubs all in NC.

Research any possible place women gather who have jobs. In the beginning it might feel vague and that is okay. Get your foot in the door. Remember you will need to contact six to seven people to get one booking or opportunity. Do a lot of research and make a big list. Keep carving away at that list daily.

2. Follow up. Email or call the contact with an initial request and let them know you will be following up. Remember pay for speaking would be great, but that is not the priority. Be thrilled to speak pro-bono to promote your business. Then, follow up appropriately until you get an answer. I am not following up to push someone for a "yes," but I am following up to get an answer, whatever that answer might be. Most people fail in the follow up.

3). Craft a killer title. Notice I said research, contact, and follow up PRIOR to crafting your speech. *Believe me, WHEN you land your first speaking gig you will write that speech very quickly.* Your primary focus should be going after the opportunities and then on crafting the message. But you should have a title ready. A killer title is one with specifics: numbers; percentages; steps and tangible benefits! Here are some great examples:

- 3 Steps to Increase Your Profits by 50% in 30 Days

- 5 Secrets to Lose 10% Body Weight and Lower Cholesterol

- 3 Ways to Discover Your Life Passion and Change Your Career This Month

4. Monetize the opportunity. When you land that first speech, you may or may not be paid. Don't sweat it. Be sure to have two things ready when you go:

- A way to collect all the names for your database. I suggest raffling off a month of your services, a spa basket, or a book depending on your target market.

- Something to offer them as a special deal if they sign up with you that evening. (i.e. your new group forming is $199 per month, but if they register today it is $149)

5. Don't be a character. The best way to speak is from the heart. Don't try to be over professional or perfect. People enjoy being inspired by people they can relate to. Have fun, bring your personality out, and tell your story. Have a good time.

Speaking can build your list fast, get people to know, like, and trust you on the spot, and you can close the sale without selling. So, go speak!

CLIENT RETENTION TIPS

In order to retain clients and build a sustainable business, you must stay in touch with people in a meaningful way. This includes people you have done business with, people you have met in person at events, and your email subscriber list.

Your client base has a sacred contract with you. They have connected, spent money and time with you. You must care enough to keep in touch with them.

Advertising experts have proven time and time again that ads that run continuously, at least three times, always outperform one-shot ad runs. The same is true with your client base. Find a way to reach them, share your message, and consistently stay connected. For coaches, consultants, healers, and other helping professionals, newsletters are one of the best ways to stay in touch. It is important to shift your mindset and action from not wanting to bother your client base, which is a common mistake that new business owners make.

"People have just given me their name. I don't want to bother them and send them things all the time." I used to say this as well. I had to recognize that touching their lives in a meaningful way allows the cream to rise to the top. Those who are truly interested in what you have to say and the solutions you offer will make themselves known to you. The rest may unsubscribe or walk away from you, but that means they really weren't engaged or dedicated to your message anyway.

Approaching marketing this way saves you time, effort, and money. Instead of chasing people who may or may not be interested or ready for your offerings, let the people who need you most identify themselves to you. Don't worry about the others. They will let you know when they are ready or simply opt-out if they are not interested.

My newsletter continually gets better readership when I write more often and when I provide a more personal touch about my family, my dog, or my travels. When I first started doing my newsletter, I did it once a month and about 35% of the people opened it and read it. Now I do my newsletter weekly, and I have sometimes up to 85% open it up and read it. It just proves that if you're consistent and really share meaningful content, people will want more of it; they will want more of you!

Newsletters are only one way to stay in touch with your clients, prospects or business contacts, but they are a great place to start. Depending on your business and the people you serve, there are dozens of other ways to touch the lives of your clients in a meaningful way.

Once you've started regularly sending out an email newsletter, consider mailing out occasional physical newsletters, cards or small gifts to show your appreciation to your clients and contacts. It done authentically and thoughtfully, investments like this will always pay off in spades.

Although there may be specific tactics and media that will work best for your business, niche, and message, the important thing is that you are consistently reaching out to your client base and prospect list in ways that show your dedication to them. Communicating how much you care through an electronic newsletter or any other method of follow up is one of the easiest and most effective ways to grow your business and increase your visibility.

THE ECONOMY OF LOVE

We live in an abundant universe. All the resources, support, and direction we need is all around. Failure is not an option in creating and growing your business—you may choose to quit, but failure is not possible with the economy of love. The Webster's definition of economy is the correct and effective use of available resources. And that is all building, marketing, and growing a business is—the effective use of your available resources.

We often attach a negative idea to resources. What words come up for you? Money, time, manpower, ideas —all the stuff that feels and seems hard.

What if I shared that your most precious and abundant resource is within you right now? It is forever present, it is the most powerful marketing tool, and it is free: LOVE.

The economy of love in your business is what you can share with those you want to help, heal, support, inspire, and serve. The truth is, this is what your clients and customers want the most of anyway. They want to feel heard, nurtured, embraced, and celebrated.

Here are three ways the economy of love is used in my business, and you can tweak it for yours, as well.

1. Be more interested than interesting.

I am all for "tooting your own horn." Actually, that is a form of love. But our clients come to us in pain or need. You will always be of higher service and greater good if you can listen to them in a deeply meaningful way. I always ask in the first session what my client's life will be like when they reach their business goal, launch their business, or meet the next money goal. I ask for two reasons:

+ 1) I am so deeply interested. I love hearing about those moments because they are their real stories. In those dreams are the opportunities to change the world.

+ 2) That really is the story they WANT to share. The hardship and hard times are what might be most on their mind, but they want to share the victory and the vision. Compassionate curiosity is the economy of love.

2. Stay in touch.

Some weeks it is not easy to write my newsletter. My assistants are always fussing at me for being a little late or behind. I want to share good ideas and I can often get caught up in perfectionism, but it always gets done because I care about you. I can't hold on to the ideas or information. It is almost too painful for me. I want to get it to you so that you can share it and change the world. I write weekly because I treat you like I would treat a good friend. I want to stay in constant touch and give you support in a timely way. Staying in touch is the economy of love.

3) Bless them and let them go:

This one is hard. In the beginning of my business, when a client left or changed their mind it would really pain me. What did I do wrong? What did I mess up? Why would they do that? It is never easy to lose a client; it means a loss of income and change. Change is hard. Those clients leave for a reason. That change happens for a higher purpose. So, now I bless them and let them go. It feels so much better, and I believe it shows myself more self-love. Nothing is wrong. Nothing is bad. It just is. So, begin to let people go when the time is right. Letting go is the economy of love.

The resource is there right now and it is abundant. What if we all used love as our greatest marketing strategy? What would our world look like? What would our business look like? And remember, LOVE is not all soft... and "yes"... and quiet. Love can be compassionate accountability, telling the truth, and some tough honesty with your clients.

ARE YOU SUPPORTING YOUR CLIENTS FULLY?

Support comes in many ways, but HOW you are supporting your clients might be truly affecting client retention and referrals. To support your clients fully, you must be 100% authentic, honest and tough.

Yes, tough. Lovingly tough.

My message about marketing is about authenticity and sharing. I truly believe that those are key to building a successful and meaningful business. Some marketers say I have a soft message with a tough delivery. And that is authentically me. As different as those may seem, it works because for me it is real.

My approach to marketing comes from compassion and my coaching style comes from massive action. What is your style? Are you tapped into your authentic self? Does your coaching and support flow from you, or do you feel like you are delivering or performing?

How you support your clients is KEY to keeping them with you and them telling others to work with you.

Here are some quick tips to support your clients authentically and fully:

1. Hold them to the Highest Standard

I expect A LOT from my clients. I expect them to show up in their lives in huge ways and bust their butts building their business, because when they don't, the people they can help don't get served. I remind them of that standard, I hold them to that standard, and I do not waiver even when I want to. I owe that to them.

2. Be the REAL You.

Your clients connect to you most when you are vulnerable, genuine, and consistent. Your style becomes your signature, and that is what makes people want more from you. I am not perfect. I have a mixed up combo of sweet and saucy, but it is all me, all the time. What is your style you can find that style just by noticing when you are in complete flow and don't even have to think about your next move.

3. Embrace Compassionate Accountability

You really fail your clients when you let them off the hook, especially when you let them off the hook over, and over, and over. Be there to help. Be there to support them in breaking through barriers, but do not let them turn excuses into reasons. Leading your clients to greatness means holding them accountable. It is the greatest expression of client caring.

Nothing is more fun and rewarding than being the real you (warts and all) so that your clients can grow and be fully supported! Sometimes it is scary to put yourself out there in that way, but you will be shocked and amazed at how the REAL you will attract more clients, move more people, and manifest more money.

6

SELLING

Here's where you'll learn my no-bullshit approach to sales.

I CARE, DO YOU?

Stop multitasking for one moment and grab a paper and a pen. Don't over process. Think from the gut.

Now, answer this question:

What is it that you would like to see changed in the world?

Write down your answer. Only give yourself 10-15 seconds. If you had a difficult time answering the question, that is the reason your business is struggling. You have to be the change you wish to see in the world. How can you grow a business around that change if you don't even know what your mission is?

When someone asks, "What do you do?" do you respond with, "Oh, I'm a life coach Reiki healer energy worker underwater basket weaver…"?

If this sounds familiar, no one knows what it is you really do. They don't care what your title is.

When you respond with your title (e.g. life coach, business coach, a Reiki master, etc.) you aren't explaining the pain you solve for people. What solution do you offer?

When someone asks me, "What is it you do?" here's what I tell people: "I work with service professionals to make more money, help more people, and have massive impact."

I don't talk about the fact that I'm coach. I don't talk about how I was trained. **Most people talk about the process of their work as opposed to the progress and results they offer**. People really don't care what your title or your training is.

Occasionally, some people will ask for your credentials or why you're able to do what you do, but for the most part, they just want to know, "Here's my problem, here's my pain, and how can you help me solve it?"

The second piece of this is, it's got to be you. **How often are you putting yourself out there and how often are you telling your story?**

When I first started my business, I was sharing my movement. I was talking to people about how I could remove, heal, and help them through their pain on a daily basis. My goal was always to talk to 100 people a week.

You may be saying, "I don't know who to talk to." That's an excuse. You do know how to reach people. **You do know how to talk to people.**

One of the first things that I suggest you do is apply what I call my one-mile radius rule (unless you live deep in the country, and then you might need to have a ten-mile radius rule). Get in your car, put on a CD, and drive all over within a one-mile radius of your house. Look at everything through the lens of, "How could I share my message?" not, "How can I get a client?" There is a difference. Focus on sharing your movement.

All of the sudden, the high school becomes an opportunity to do an expo or to teach at their adult education school. The diner with the Rotary Club sign becomes a place to speak. Businesses in your community become places to contact. The church, the community center—I could go on and on.

Everything you need to build a multiple-6-figure business is within a one-mile radius of your home. You can have all the websites in the world, you can have the marketing materials, you can have all of that, but **if you are not talking to at least 100 people a week, then you are not reaching enough people.**

Once you are talking to people or reaching them in other ways, there is a possibility that you don't know how to convert, which means you have a selling problem. You may be too salesy or you may not be selling at all.

The process for converting people into clients is called my "I CARE" system. It's a five-step process.

"I CARE" stands for:

> **I**nspire
> **C**larify
> **A**sk
> **R**eceive
> **E**mbrace

If you are talking to enough people and still not making sales, you have an authenticity problem. This means you're not bringing enough of you into it. When you don't bring enough of you into it, you either are scared to death to sell at all, or you're overselling and not being your authentic self.

HOW TO SELL WITH LOVE

You aren't really in business if you aren't selling. The transformation is actually IN the sale. I know many people are really concerned about feeling pushy, hard, or aggressive. As I've said before, there is one easy key that makes sales fun, easy, and profitable : LOVE!

Remember that sales is something you do for people and not something you do to people. You have gifts to share and in those gifts you have the "answer" or "solution" people need for their pain. If you don't make the decision to love your clients and prospects then you can't help them. Most people say their dream is not based in money, but meaning, helping, and serving. I agree! But you can only help people in a limited way if you are not asking for the sale. Here are some easy ways to LOVE 'EM UP:

1. REMEMBER "WHY!" Why do you do what you do? Are you really here to give back? Giving back means giving people the opportunity to invest in themselves and grow.

2. REMEMBER "WHAT!" There is honor and strength in asking for money. In other words, having people pay for your services gives them skin in the game. And there is no better investment in the world than the investment in you. Don't take that opportunity away from clients.

3. REMEMBER "WHERE!" Please don't judge people, places or opportunities of the correctness to sale. You will be surprised where people will find you and where you can find people. You share your messages and gifts where you can and don't judge opportunities—especially in the beginning. Just get your message out!

4. REMEMBER "WHEN!" The time is now. YOUR job is to get potential clients to make a decision—not to say, "Yes." Just remember that not everyone is meant to work with you, but the most difficult thing for people to do is decide. You have to hold the space for that. Whether the answer is a "hell yes" or a "hell no," love them to a decision.

5. REMEMBER "WITH!" With love and caring for people, you can make more money and a bigger difference. What beliefs do you lead WITH? Do you believe your mission is to help people? Do you believe that by selling you serve? Do you believe selling is nothing more than sharing? Notice the beliefs you lead with.

Think about changing your sales language. The next time you have a sales call or conversation, tell yourself that you are going to love them to the "YES!" Selling is nothing more than love. And I know this is why you do what you do, to love people so that love gets paid forward. So, love people and watch your world and their world transform all through the SALE.

WHAT DOES YOUR RATE SAY ABOUT YOU?

Once you have people coming into your pipeline through a coherent and multi-faceted lead generation strategy you must set a rate that doesn't repel people, but instead attracts people.

Most people I encounter fall into one of two camps:

1. They are undercharging by a considerable amount.

2. They have no idea what to charge at all and they feel lost.

So, I'm going address this common issue for entrepreneurs right now. Let's make this simple.

Grab a piece of paper and write down what you think you should charge. For this exercise, make it an hourly rate. Don't think about it too hard, just write it down.

Now I want you to double that number.

Somewhere in between that initial number and the doubled version is what your actual rate should be. You can take an average of the two numbers if you want to make it simple, and you're set.

This new rate will start you off, but it certainly won't be the rate that you'll have forever. As you grow, you should be raising your rate appropriately.

You don't want to have a rate that is so low that people say, "Hmmm...does this person know what they are doing?"

Write this down: Your rate is an announcement to the world of your confidence in your skill set.

When you tell people your rate, what are you saying about yourself? You must establish a rate that is meaningful and that really represents you as an expert in your field.

Beyond that simple hourly rate, you should have a menu of services. Too many coaches, consultants, healers and other entrepreneurs only offer one thing.

If you went to an Italian restaurant and the only thing they had was spaghetti, even if you loved spaghetti, I doubt you'd go back there again. Not everyone going with you may like spaghetti. They may want something a little bit different. You must have a menu.

On the other hand, don't create a menu of services that is extremely large or complex. If you have 20 different items or services, it might be so confusing that it will overwhelm people.

You should start with about three packages. Why? Most people don't like to make decisions!

When offered three choices, they will usually go with the middle package. At convenience stores, the #1 drink size chosen is the middle one. People think, 'The small one may not be enough, but the big one looks too large, so I'll pick the middle one."

Having 3 packages helps people make a decision. Generally people will feel safe and comfortable with the middle package.

So the key points to remember when evaluating your rates are:

◆ Don't undercharge. Remember that your rate is a statement to the world of your confidence in your skill set.

◆ Continually re-evaluate your rate and make changes when appropriate.

◆ Have a menu of services with optimally around three main programs at different price points.

7

MAKING MONEY

Guess what? I'm about to give you the greatest gift in the world. (No, not free money wiseass.)

I'm about to show you why that if you're serious about changing the world, you've got to make money. Bring a pen and paper.

CHANGE YOUR BANK ACCOUNT TO CHANGE THE WORLD

You have heard me say it before, but here we go again: The more money you make, the more people you can help.

It's true.

My mentor says that money is not the most important thing in the world, but it touches everything that is. Money is the great equalizer; it brings equality. I was never as clear about this as when I was in Africa. Money allows you to be truly free, and ultimate financial freedom allows you to help others be free. Most of you reading this know that our passions go beyond earning money, but let me make a bold statement here:

My passion is making money.

I know I can turn that revenue or profit into opportunity. Education brings entrepreneurship, which brings equality. Every dollar I make lets me do something more, better, or bigger for myself and others and every ounce of that trickles up and down to play a role in the cycle of opportunity.

There is no shame in making money.

There is no shame in asking for money.

There is no shame in being focused on money.

There is no shame in making money important.

On occasion I will get an email chastising me for being focused on profits and reminding me that my motto is, "help more people," as if helping more people and making money are separate. They are the most connected of any two actions. If you truly want to help more people, you will want to make more money just as passionately. Here are some keys to making a big difference:

1. Ask for money. Your gift is your gift because you are meant to share it and be rewarded, and those rewards are meant for your abundance and generosity to others.

2. Stop confusing giving back with giving it away. When you give your services away you don't help anyone. You lose the value and the opportunity to create revenue that you can use to contribute.

3. Let go of the shame. God did not intend for us to be broke or worry about money. Just look at the Universe. The blade of grass does not struggle to grow. The environment is abundant with air to breathe. Money worry is a choice. You always get what you need when you need it.

4. Make it a priority to make as much money as you absolutely can. And then be armed and ready to change your world and the world around you. I am motivated to educate girls. I am motivated to cultivate entrepreneurs. I am committed to bringing equality. It will take money, so I am fine with making more and making it a focus.

Money is the great equalizer. Wanna change the world? Change your bank account.

HERE'S MY PLAN FOR MONEY

Most business owners have a passion, a good idea, or a skill and get inspired to monetize. That's always the seed of a great start-up. Where most start-ups fail is they believe that their passion will bring them the money. Passion will inspire you to work hard and get you out of bed in the morning, but it is not a plan. You need a solid plan, and it needs to be based in 10% information and 90% implementation.

When you have a plan, you are able to scale your model and profit centers become rinse and repeat. Here is the 5-step plan I follow to make money—every day, every time.

1. Ask, "Where?" When you plan a project, launch, or product, know from the start where you want it to take you both financially and in terms of positioning. It is key to have an overall plan for the year so you understand the impact every launch or idea has. Most people simply throw the spaghetti on the wall and hope something sticks. But it is imperative that you ask where this is going to take you and have a clear and measurable outcome.

2. Ask, "When?" What are your set dates for the most successful profit outcome? Once you determine those, you have to live and die by them. When you miss launch dates, you throw off your entire profit cycle.

3. Ask, "Who?" Loral Langmeir had a phenomenal quote: "When an opportunity comes to you, ask yourself the million-dollar question: Who can I get to do this for me?" You must leverage your time as soon as possible (even if you are just starting out). Have a team of resources, contractors, or employees to carry out the tasks and technical work so you can do what you do best.

4. Analyze and test. Everything I do is a test—every email, call, newsletter, or event. We are constantly analyzing our results and improving upon what worked, changing what did not, and eliminating waste. You market in a vacuum if you don't analyze and test your results from start to finish.

5. Play big and plan small. Most companies are focused on the big end result or the 3-5 year plan. They become so consumed with the big picture that they can't figure out what to do right now. Don't plan further out than 60 days for doable step-by-step, sustainable results that can be tested. Your results truly are indicators of which next step to take. Nano planning allows for flexibility and achievable results.

Hope is not a business plan, nor is passion. Those items just enable you to work the plan. If you need to increase revenues, start with these simple steps and when you explode your profits. Here is the good news: These steps still apply. Rinse and repeat.

THE FASTEST PATH TO AUTHENTIC INCOME

In business, there needs to be a systematic way to grow your income and your money mountain. It is easy to "chase the paper," in the words of Jay-Z, but it can be exhausting. There are so many things being thrown at us today as money-makers, such as audio, video, teleclasses, podcasting, social media...I could go on and on. We become excited and obsessed with the latest "gadget" to market and we lose sight of our own mission because we're focused on the latest marketing trick.

Money and clients are ready, willing, and waiting for you now. You don't need to put on fancy bells or ad whistles to make more money. You actually need to go back to the basics. Go back to what inspired you to start your business and share your gift. Go back to what you already know, have and are. Put YOU back in the process. Clients call me wanting to coach and are ready to focus on tactics to get clients or dig into creating another product.

Before you start creating, developing, and running the marketing rat race, slow down and start here:

◆ **Focus on Active before Passive.**

Get active income going in your business ASAP. Active is where you are "doing" the work: coaching a client; having a session; leading a group; etc. Then you can move into passive income. Passive income is where you might sell a book, product, or program that does not involve your time. Passive income typically requires a larger list and a deeper reach. I am all for passive income. It's very important, but only AFTER you have active income, so that you are nurturing relationships, referrals, and your visibility.

◆ **Look around You.**

We often get so busy with the latest marketing trend that we forget to check our backyard for opportunities. Have you emailed friends, family, and associates? Have you set up coffee with people in your circle of influence? Have you had a house party and invited people over for a mini workshop or seminar? Don't forget the opportunities from people who already know, like, and trust you.

◆ **Ask, "What is within one mile?"**

Make a list of all networking and visibility opportunities within about one mile of your home. Okay, if you live in the country or deep woods, maybe change this to 10 miles. Write down churches, schools, cafes, doctor offices, and community groups... Seriously, do this exercise. Get in your car and drive around for 20 minutes.

Look at everything as a potential place to speak, network, and share your business. (Heads up: This is a very brief explanation of what I cover in the "I Care…do you? Chapter. So if you've been skipping around and want to read up on this, please go back and check it out)

◆ **Write.**

Maybe getting out of the house is not that easy for you, or you live in an area where it is difficult to reach civilization. Then WRITE! Seek out places to be a guest blogger, guest newsletter writer or article market. Post on forums and use your email like you mean it. Write about your work everywhere and anywhere you can.

◆ **Cold Call.**

I know. THE. DIRTY. WORD. What I mean is cold calling with purpose. Could you call former clients and ask for referrals? Call friends and brainstorm marketing opportunities. Certainly call places to speak, from the local library to the Chamber, to the associations within your market. I tell you, making 5-targeted calls a day WILL grow your business.

◆ **Focus on Movement over Marketing**

Go back to what matters. Your mission, your meaning, and your purpose IS what sells. The fastest path to authentic income is realigning with your WHY. It is what attracts people to work with you.

Accelerating our income becomes elusive when we lose sight of the resources we already have available to us. So breathe and take a step back. Clients, business, and income are all around you. Reach out and grab it so you can help more people.

EARN MORE WITH YOUR ENVIRONMENT

Your income is directly tied to your environment.

Take a pause. Look around you right now. Also, quickly jot down the 5 people you spend the most time with. The space you create for yourself is the mirror to your income and business potential. One of my Soul Business Sisters, Tamra says that she loves helping people create a space that is a reflection of their soul. Often, we do that naturally. Who and what is around us is a pretty good indication of what's going on inside us and how we value ourselves.

Our income, our environment, and our business are all based in choices. You can turn your environment—and thus your income—around just as quickly as you turn a light switch on or off. I have often found that when I feel a bit stuck in marketing or business growth, I really need to be working on my surroundings. I need to be up-leveling. And yes, anytime we move ourselves into more abundance, joy, and beauty, we must leave something behind. We always exchange something of a lower nature for a higher nature. So, maybe you don't need to be marketing this week. Maybe you need to be expanding the potential of the space and people around you. Try these quick tips:

1. Expand your reach. We are the average of the five people we spend the most time with. I know the concept can be a difficult one to understand (because we all have best friends and family and loved ones), but the time spent with those who don't help you to stretch and push your boundaries keeps you stuck. You may need to let some people go or just bring more abundant, juicy, positive people into your life. When you up-level the people around you, your income and joy will up-level. Remember the Rule of Five.

2. Smell the Roses. We often forget the smell sense and how it can have a massive effect on our mood and energy. I love Young Living Essential Oils, and I can take my mind, motivation, and mojo anywhere fast by shifting the sense of smell. My favorites are Lavender, Peace and Calming, Envision, and Peppermint.

Remember, everything we breathe, taste, touch, or see affects our earnings.

3. See the Roses. Flowers are luxurious and they can change the mood of any space. Maybe you can put fresh flowers on your desk, or position your office so that you can see flowers or trees outside. Either way, your confidence is raised when you see beauty because you feel beautiful. Is your office and workspace beautiful?

4. Clear out the clutter. Money is energy and it must have space to travel. Some ways it does NOT travel well is through stacks of paper, piles of clothes, or disorganized and unused files. Find huge chunks of open space and air to let all the good stuff to come in.

And no excuses... if this simple thought overwhelms you or scares the heck out of you, contact a personal organizer.

5. First Class. Travel first class—air, hotel, meals. I know you might say, "THAT is not where I can spend my money right now." And believe me, I know what you mean. I thought that was a luxury reserved for millionaires and billionaires, but I discovered that it actually doesn't cost THAT much more, and it has changed my life. I can travel with ease, and no matter where I go, my surroundings remain abundant and exciting. When you up-level, your income up-levels every time.

Your environment reflects your income. What is yours saying? Success is all about choices. So simply choose differently for today.

These are easy to implement and fun! This week, try a little mood marketing.

HOW TO MAKE A MILLION DOLLARS

There's no secret to making a million dollars.

It's the process of making a dollar, a million times. It's just up to you how that happens. You can do it a dollar at a time, five dollars at a time, or a hundred thousand at a time.

Regardless, it's the same process.

8

QUITTING

Quitting is lame.

It's true.

Especially since most people quit right before they reach the really good stuff.

THE ONE STRATEGY THAT DOESN'T GET SAID

It is the most extraordinary experience.

Watching clients and colleagues.

Watching where they stop.

Watching how they stop.

I see it over. And over. And over again.

Write this one down please: Temporary Defeat = I Quit.

I share this idea in almost every newsletter, but that is because it is the most important concept you will ever embrace. And it is simple.

If you want to succeed, make more money, help more people, or have more of an impact, keep going! Ignore the outcomes, setbacks, and no shows. Keep going! THIS is my secret. People keep asking how I did it. The secret is this, and it is how I continue to do it:

1. I keep going in every situation.

2. I stay focused on the dream and visions and not on the how or temporary outcome.

3. I get the right help when I need it. I seek out the right mentors. I do not do it alone.

4. I keep going in every situation (Repeated intentionally).

This is my favorite story in Napoleon Hill's Think and Grow Rich. Read it once and then over again. Is this where you are? What will your next step be?

"One of the most common causes of failure is the habit of quitting when one is overtaken by temporary defeat. Every person is guilty of this mistake at one time or another. An uncle of R. U. Darby was caught by the 'gold fever' in the gold-rush days, and went west to DIG AND GROW RICH. He had never heard that more gold has been mined from the brains of men than has ever been taken from the earth. He staked a claim and went to work with pick and shovel. The going was hard, but his lust for gold was definite.

After weeks of labor, he was rewarded by the discovery of the shining ore. He needed machinery to bring the ore to the surface. Quietly, he covered up the mine, retraced his footsteps to his home in Williamsburg, Maryland, told his relatives and a few neighbors of the 'strike.'

They got together money for the needed machinery, had it shipped. The uncle and Darby went back to work the mine.

The first car of ore was mined, and shipped to a smelter. The returns proved they had one of the richest mines in Colorado! A few more cars of that ore would clear the debts. Then would come the big killing in profits.

Down went the drills! Up went the hopes of Darby and Uncle! Then something happened! The vein of gold ore disappeared! They had come to the end of the rainbow, and the pot of gold was no longer there! They drilled on, desperately trying to pick up the vein again all to no avail.

Finally, they decided to QUIT. They sold the machinery to a junk man for a few hundred dollars, and took the train back home. Some 'junk' men are dumb, but not this one! He called in a mining engineer to look at the mine and do a little calculating. The engineer advised that the project had failed, because the owners were not familiar with 'fault lines.' His calculations showed that the vein would be found JUST THREE FEET FROM WHERE THE DARBYS HAD STOPPED DRILLING! That is exactly where it was found!

The 'Junk' man took millions of dollars in ore from the mine, because he knew enough to seek expert counsel before giving up. Most of the money that went into the machinery was procured through the efforts of R.

U. Darby, who was then a very young man. The money came from his relatives and neighbors, because of their faith in him. He paid back every dollar of it, although he was years in doing so.

Long afterward, Mr. Darby recouped his loss many times over, when he made the discovery that DESIRE can be transmuted into gold. The discovery came after he went into the business of selling life insurance.

Remembering that he lost a huge fortune, because he STOPPED three feet from gold, Darby profited by the experience in his chosen work, by the simple method of saying to himself, 'I stopped three feet from gold, but I will never stop because men say `no' when I ask them to buy insurance.'

Darby is one of a small group of fewer than fifty men who sell more than a million dollars in life insurance annually. He owes his 'stickability' to the lesson he learned from his "quitability" in the gold mining business.

Before success comes in any man's life, he is sure to meet with much temporary defeat, and, perhaps, some failure. When defeat overtakes a man, the easiest and most logical thing to do is to QUIT. That is exactly what the majority of men do.

More than five hundred of the most successful men this country has ever known, told the author their greatest success came just one step beyond the point at which defeat had overtaken them. Failure is a trickster with a keen sense of irony and cunning. It takes great delight in tripping one when success is almost within reach."

Now is not the time to give up! Keep going, ask for help, and change the world.

◆

It takes many skills to grow, sustain, and build a business. Everything from marketing, to mindset, to math has to be in play to make real money and a real difference. All the education, time, and money you have put into growing your business won't much matter if you don't embody this: tenacity!

Never give up. Never quit.

People always want to know how I did it, and what the one big shift was that happened.

It's simple.

I didn't stop. I didn't stop when…

People said No.

I ran out of money.

I got tired.

I went dry creatively.

Someone hurt my feelings.

Someone no showed.

People discouraged me.

I felt I wasn't enough.

I was told I wasn't enough.

The clients I did have left.

No one new came.

The car broke down.

A family member died.

I was confused.

I was scared.

I didn't stop.

The greatest business skill set you need is tenacity. All the other stuff just makes this path easier. Tenacity makes the path possible.

Now, here's what you do.

When the money runs out...Get a job! (I like to call it a "business loan.") Fund your dream. If you believe in it enough, find the income stream to support it.

When people leave... Find new people! Clients leave for a reason. They are often afraid of success, and some leave because they are complete. Let them go, take a breath, and ASK; find new people to share your message. Don't stop.

When you are scared... Go through it! The only way out is through. There is no magic pill. There is no step-by-step system for fear. When you do it, it gets easier... when you build that muscle, you get braver.

Courage is a learned skill.

When you get tired... Ask for help! No man is an island. I didn't build this alone, and neither can you. You need to only work in your brilliance and delegate the rest.

When someone hurts your feelings... Remember who you are! I didn't get in this business to make friends. I do this to make a difference. Not everyone will like me, my style, or my methods. There are other coaches for them. I know who I am.

When you feel you aren't enough... Know the truth. You are a child of God. You are here to let your light shine and you are enough. If you are reading this, it means you believe in possibility. Share that possibility, for it is love.

Tenacity is the only business skill you ever need to know.

GO TO THE "YES"

When in business for yourself, you succeed by getting "yes"es: "Yes, I want to be your client." "Yes, you can speak." "Yes, you can write an article for us." "Yes, you can join my group." It is the "yes" that excites us and makes us money! The "yes" enables us to help more people.

I realize that we do get a lot of "no"s. The most successful entrepreneurs get more "no"s than "yes"es, and that's mainly because they are moving toward the "yes"es with more veracity. It needs to become a valuable moment to land that "no." It means you are putting yourself out there in a big way and you are seeking opportunity.

Too many times, entrepreneurs wait. They want the time to be right, the idea to be perfect, and the approach to feel authentic. I understand all these desires, but the most authentic you can be is showing up every day and going after the "yes."

Recently, I have known there are things I want to accomplish and the answers I need are hard to come by. But I also know there will never be a perfect way or a perfect time so the only way to grow a business is to dive in. You have to go to the "YES."

Here are a few ways I built my business and wake up every day heading toward "YES!"

1. Google.

I research five to ten speaking opportunities for organizations or groups and send them five to ten emails a day.

2. Have a plan.

The minute you get a "no", it can be discouraging. You need to plan what your next step is so that you can move on and keep marketing.

3. Have a big-thinking mentor.

When I am thinking too small, I make certain to turn to my mentor and mastermind members to kick my ass a little. You need to have the right mentor to help you towards the "YES."

4. Ask anyway.

Often, we assume something will not work, a group will not want our workshop, or the client can't afford us. Nothing has served me better than to ASK anyway.

5. See the "no"s as stepping-stones.

Every time I get a "no," I get closer to a "yes." The "no"s are like overtures; they warm up the audience for the main event.

What's the event? It's the "YES! Stop worrying about rejection and get excited to put yourself out there in a big way!" event.

Now say, "Yes," and go make it happen!

9

MEDITATIONS ON THE "RIGHT TIME"

If you're one of those people who say they want to wait until "the right time" to do anything, here's some good news:

The right time is right now.

DON'T WAIT UNTIL THE TIME IS RIGHT

I often get told that someone is waiting to start their business or one of my programs, or to make a change until the time is right. Without being disrespectful, it is laughable. It is laughable for a few reasons: First, it is laughable to believe that we actually have this much control. Second, it is laughable to believe that you are delaying your destiny out of integrity. And third, if you have thought about something even for a nanosecond, then the time to act on it is now.

Accurate thinking will tell you that life is just a series of moments, and the more you wait, well, the more you wait. I know it seems simple, but that's because it is. I don't think there is a right time for someone to die any more than there is a right time for someone to be born. I don't think you meditate or ponder the right time to launch a business or get the help you need.

You feel and then do it.

Yep, you might think that can get you in trouble. Feel it, do it, and don't think it. I will tell you the trouble it has gotten me in is the best kind. I was moving forward. And maybe I looked a little foolish or wasn't quite ready, but the payoff was action. The reward was no more waiting.

I know some of you are scared, and that's why it doesn't seem like the right time. I feel you. Fear is the biggest factor in waiting. Fear will always make you wonder.

So, for those who have ever wanted off my list when I've told you to get off your ass, I wonder why that struck you so deeply. Have you been sitting on your rear a bit too long?

◆ And for those who started a program and quit or didn't follow through, I wonder why you forgot that I believed in you until could the moment you believed in yourself.

◆ For those who have blamed others for not making the money they wanted or having the success they desire, I wonder who hurt you that you have not yet forgiven.

◆ And for those who said, "Next time, I will get the support I need, but for now I am not ready," why do you not see your magnificent possibility?

◆ For those who want to change the world, I ask you, are you willing to first change YOUR world?

There is only one right time. And you are living in it as you read th is. At the end of this chapter, go make the boldest decision you have ever made. This is the right time, and you have my love, confidence, and support.

Go do it and then come back. I'll be here.

THE SECRET TO FAILURE

Let me just spill the beans for you: Business success has almost nothing to do with business know-how and everything to do with mindset. The marketing pieces can be learned, and sometimes you can even delegate small parts of them out. But the deep core belief that it takes to manifest a BIG business is your central key to success.

You can think what you want, but if your business dream is not where you had imagined it would be, all the details in the world will not push you through to business success. I know, because I have tried it. I have tried to do everything right and get all my marketing ducks in a row, but if my belief about what is possible for me was out of alignment, all those tools just sat there. Nothing much happened.

It's easy to blame everything else when things aren't going your way: "I don't have a website or a team." "I don't know where to market or how to write sales copy." All of that pales in the shadow of what you DO believe is possible for your business!

"You can never earn in the outside world more than you earn in your own mind." —Brian Tracy

You have to get a picture-perfect, clear image of where you can be in 3 months, 6 months, or a year. And then with every daily action and every decision you make, the foundation must be that you KNOW this is where you are headed.

Entrepreneurship is not for the weak. I know most of you are deep-feeling, caring, giving people. The giving has to start with YOU! What do you believe for yourself? What stories of defeat do you keep whispering in your own ear?

The only reason you will not succeed is because of the story you are telling yourself. I wish you could see YOU from the view I have—all the hope, possibilities, brilliance, power, and talent. Take that image and use it for the fuel to do your best work. You cannot help more people living in the "what if"s and "maybe"s.

What is your success story?

10

IN CLOSING

Here are some finishing thoughts on everything I've shared in the preceding pages and some ways to take action if you want to get on the path to 7 figures.

THIS ALMOST RUINED ME

I had this delusion that there was a finish line in business. I had thought that I would hustle, build my reputation, fill my practice, fill my bank account, and watch it start to go on autopilot.

Ah, nope.

Now, don't get me wrong. We have systematized and automated much in my business. But the truth is there is no finish line. There is no moment when you kick back and watch it all happen. Now that I think back, I am not even sure why I wanted things to go that way. Maybe I was tired from my job, or dreaming of doing nothing for just a little while. When I say it now, it seems silly. I love what I do. Why would I want to do nothing?

But, so many people email me and say they can't wait to be where I am. They can't wait to sit back and have made it.

I now know that is the kiss of death. None of this is about "making it" or money. It is all about the journey. The minute the journey stops, the minute you get comfortable, the minute you stand at the finish line, you are finished. I think the finish line could have ruined me in business. What would there be to learn from, grow into, or stretch?

Trust me. You don't want a finish line.

I think what you really want is not to struggle, and that is accurate thinking. Struggle is optional. Effort is required. Life is richer when you are in the race (not the rat race) and you are running to beat your last best time.

What you really want is to be asking yourself, "What can I do to reach my fullest potential today, and how can I help others reach theirs?" The minute you live into the truth that this will never be "done," money will follow. You have to embrace the continual process of work. Work is not a dirty word.

The definition of work is, physical or mental effort or activity directed toward the production or accomplishment of something.

I like that.

Give me that life. To wake up every day and make effort for the

accomplishment of something good. Take it from me : Eliminate the delusion of the finish line. You'll be happier and you'll get more done.

FAT, GAY, AND BROKE

May I be the first to point out my obvious obstacles? Some just may surprise you:

Yep, I am overweight.

Yep, I am gay.

Yep, I was broke.

And I had no business skills, was unsure of my purpose, and was working over 60 hours a week in a day job. I had excuses. I had obstacles. I had a potty mouth and I am really opinionated. While growing the business I also lost three family members. I lost team members. I can't use technology. I was in debt big time, too.

I am sure I have left some things out, but here it is, all in one big list for all to see. Something on the list may even offend you, but the list is me in all the truth, vulnerability, and imperfection.

You either do it, or you don't. All the business building, marketing classes, social media spin-offs, and mindset adjustments in the world will not help you make money or make a difference if you decide to let the obstacles be in control. If you choose excuses and blame over action, you will stay stuck. If you choose what's wrong over what's possible, it will be impossible.

Ask yourself where you fall. Ask yourself the real heart of the WHY you aren't where you want to be. And how many people, reasons, and obstacles are you blaming? I had to do it. I had to do it no matter what, because I wasn't going to live this life playing small. I wasn't going to live this life not having lived my dreams. I want the same for you: I want you to do it despite your circumstances. I want you to do it despite your situation.

Life is unpredictable.

All your plans will change.

You will fail. And you can get back up.

If I can do it fat, gay, and broke, you can do it.

Go change the world, but start by changing yours. If you are waiting to be perfect, you are actually keeping people from an experience of learning from you now and just the way you are. Your flaws are your relevance, and your obstacles are your guideposts to success. Stop cursing the pain of growth and change. Start celebrating that you can feel it and that you are living it. If in this moment you are comfortable, then you aren't stretching big enough.

Take a "no excuses" approach. There is no other way to make this all work.

YOU MAY HAVE FORGOTTEN

"Success means having the courage, the determination and the will to become the person you believe you were meant to be."—George Sheehan

- Feeling like the marketing is hard?

- A little blue because you lost a client?

- Can't seem to get motivated or on track?

- Not sure you are meant to be in business?

You forgot.

Yes, YOU forgot.

You are not a series of disappointments. You are not marketing, websites, and hard work. You are not the answers you get, nor the answers you give.

YOU are a gift.

—a gift to share with others. And if you are standing knee deep in your own worry, fear, self-pity, or disappointment, then you are not living your highest purpose. All the swirling "stuff" that is weighing you down is just that—TUFF. It actually has very little to do with you. But, you may be at a point right now where you are allowing it to become YOU.

It breaks my heart when I get emails/calls from people who are bursting with possibility and purpose, yet can't make the quantum leap. Their reasons are always the same: "Not enough."

Not enough...

- ◆ Money

- ◆ Time

- ◆ Support

- ◆ Training

- ◆ Family

And it never has anything to do with the above.

Please write this down somewhere:

We always find the time, money, and resources to do what we truly want to do.

We always do. This might feel uncomfortable or even make you a bit annoyed. That is how I felt about it—for a while, too.

It's okay. You just forgot. You simply forgot that you are talented, needed, gifted, beautiful, inspiring, smart, abundant, and brave.

You forgot that building a business is not a dream; it is your purpose.

You forgot that you are not the no's, nor the yeses. You are the NOW. You are the divine intention you have to make a difference and make meaning.

It's okay.

I am happy to remind you. Now, YOU have to own it. Stand up from your computer right now and embrace all the possibility and abundance. When you forget again (and we all do), see me and my team.

We have enough belief for ALL of you! And it keeps flowing. The belief is abundant, plentiful, and never ending.

HAVE YOU LOST CLIENTS OR MONEY?

Biz works in flow. Clients flow in & out. Same with money. If you are in a rut—cool! The next turn is an upturn. Don't be bummed; be excited!

As we draw to a close, I want to share some thoughts you must remember in this game:

◆ What goes up must come down.

◆ We must let go of something of a lower nature to get something of a higher nature.

◆ Life is a circle. What seems like the end may actually be the beginning.

Choose any of the above to remind yourself that nothing moves in one direction continuously. Everything needs waves, flow, and rest. When I embraced the knowledge of what I call the "exodus"—many clients leaving at once or cash flow taking a quick shift—everything changed for me. I used to think, "What am I doing wrong? Why is this all happening at once? How do I save this?"

Now, I realize, you don't need to save everyone and everything. The flow is meant to be. Clients leave to make space for new, more ideal clients. Income evaporates to create the opening for a renewed, more abundant amount from a source more in alignment with your heart. Opportunities disappear because they would eventually take too much of your time or energy for little payoff. People fade away because they were not holding your dreams for you. Their fear made your fear deeper.

I know some of you are feeling this; I have felt it and still do at times. WHY the exodus of money, funds, people, opportunities? Just take a moment and pause.

Get clear.

What is around the corner? What new, fresh, inspiring opportunity is present? What opening is being formed to be filled with more money and more life? What may feel like sacrifice now is the formation of future opportunity.

Let it go. Let it flow. What may seem like the end is really just the beginning.

CHEAP CHEAP CHEAP

Business is expensive. It takes investment, time, commitment, and effort. Do you know the business owner who won't go to the networking event because they have to pay for parking or breakfast or travel?

You do. You may have even been one.

My mentor, David, says, "There is no convenient time or place to become successful." I love this, because it is exactly how I built my business—by going to the "YES!" The "yes" does not come to you, knock on the door, and deliver a payday. This quote has been on my radar for the last three weeks, so I thought I better share:

"Opportunity is missed by most people because it's dressed in overall, & looks like work." —Thomas A. Edison

So, here's the deal—I am gonna lay it out fast and dirty. Get this right and you can get millions.

Here are all the places not to be cheap, so you don't attract cheap:

1. Don't get a cheap mentor. Okay, do I have to say anything else? It seems obvious: Cheap gets you cheap. Ever think, "If this mentor is so good, why do they charge so little?" You should.

2. Don't get cheap business cards. I always forget my biz cards. (Okay, I'll be honest. I don't use them anymore.) But if you are going to have them, have them say, "Expensive."

3. Don't go networking or speaking in cheap clothes. I cannot tell you how many smart, savvy, fun people I meet who, while they are speaking to me, totally distract me because they look as if they have put absolutely no effort in showing up as their best self. I don't pretend to be a fashionista. But I want to look my best, feel my best, and show up as my best self.

4. Don't be cheap with your resources. Give away your best, and they will buy the rest. Seriously. I hate when people tease you in the attempt to make more money. If you stand by your services, are great at what you do, and love people up, they will want more.

5. Don't be cheap with your time. Business takes effort. When I hear people say they don't want to work hard, I am clear on their best path. Get a job. Business takes hustle, and if you love what you do, it won't feel like work. Being cheap with your time will get you cheap results.

Find a rich mentor. Deliver rich resources and results. Invest richly in your business and you will reap rich rewards!

A BUSINESS BUILT ON FAITH

When growing your business, it's not about LUCK; it's about FAITH. How much do you have? Let me give you some examples of what I mean:

◆ When we get on a plane, we have the FAITH it is going to fly!

◆ When we go to bed, we have FAITH that in the morning there will be light!

◆ When we leave our house, we have the FAITH that it will be there when we return.

90% of our daily activities are solely based on our faith and belief. If we had no faith, we wouldn't even be able to get out of bed in the morning. Faith fuels our very being. Yet when it comes to getting clients and building our business, it seems that there is a faith shortage.

If we hold a workshop and one person shows, then we tell ourselves we have the wrong niche. If the first 10 people we speak to say, "No" to our service, we convince ourselves that we hate marketing. Where is the faith? A good friend shared this wonderful analogy with me this weekend about business building:

"If am handed 10,000 oyster shells and told 10 have a million-dollar pearl...

I begin to open them. Phew. Oysters are hard to open.

I try 1, 2, 3, 4. No pearl. Shit. 5, 6… I cut my hand. This is really hard.

Now I'm up to 7, 8, 9, 10 … Still no pearl. So frustrating.

This is a stupid idea! There are no pearls in any of these! I hate oysters! I don't even want a million dollars!"

And before you know it, there is no faith.

Faith is tested when things get hard, when we are afraid, and when our perfectly-laid plans aren't so perfect. True faith is continued belief in the face of adversity. True faith is when you have every single reason in the world to have NO faith, especially in business.

So, here is how you hold on and keep faith the center of your business development:

1. Be clear about what you want. Faith wavers when it is uncertain what to claim. Claim what you want.

2. Stop being realistic.

3. Stop looking for the results. It is not your job. They will come. Your job is faith, action, repeat.

4. Know that our faith will be constantly tested. You pass the test when you continue to believe.

"Faith isn't faith until it's all you're holding on to."
—Anonymous

No business was ever built on uncertainty, and no leader appeared out of doubt.

THERE ARE NO CINDERELLA STORIES

In college basketball, the term, "Cinderella Story," is often used for the underdog who comes out of nowhere to win the prize. It is a romantic idea about rising from the ashes and winning the prince or prize.

Ponder what it takes to win a championship or bring home a gold medal.

- How many early morning training sessions?

- Pulled muscles?

- Wins?

- Losses?

- How much money saved?

- How much money spent?

- How many heartbreaks?

- Days when you couldn't go on?

- Days when you knew you could do it?

It's amazing what goes into a WIN!

What does it take? Some of it is obvious: hard work; commitment; dedication; etc. But what isn't so obvious?

WILL. It's hard to see will

So ask yourself:

- What do you really want for your life and business?

- What are you WILLING to sacrifice? Do? Be? Try?

- How WILLING are you to fail?

- How WILLING are you to try something new?

- How WILLING are you to leave others behind so you can grow?

- How WILLING are you to get up again?

- What are you WILLING to stop doing?

- What are you WILLING to start?

On my desk I have a little handmade sign that reads:

THERE ARE NO CINDERELLA STORIES

And there aren't. I look at this picture every day.

Magic and manifestation are the principles I operate from, but WILL is my highest value.

(WHY THERE IS NO) "THE END"

Traditionally, when you come to the final pages of most books you may find yourself greeted with the famed expression "The End" which signifies the completion of the story or the culmination of the big ideas shared within a text.

This book has no such thing.

Why? Because business has no end, either.

The truth is that business is a marathon—an ongoing endurance race with no clear cut finish line or end point. This may terrify those of you who are sitting there desperately hoping to see two people at the finish line holding ribbon as you run across it.

That's just not going to happen. And I truly hope that this inspires most of you. Life only stops the day you die and your business only stops the day you stop taking action.

So rather than view your business as a book that will one day be finished, instead view it as a journal that you are constantly adding chapters to.

It is my belief that your greatest chapter has yet to be written. So get off your ass now and get going.

Hell Yeah.